ACHIEVING

EYPS

Validation Process for EYPS

ACHIEVING
EYPS

The Validation Process for EYPS

JENNIFER COLLOBY

Series editors: Gill Goodliff and Lyn Trodd

LearningMatters

First published in 2008 by Learning Matters Ltd

British Library Cataloguing in Publication Data
A CIP record for this book is available from the British Library

ISBN 978 1 84445 1265

Cover design by Phil Barker
Text design by Code 5 Design Associates Ltd
Project Management by Swales & Willis Ltd, Exeter, Devon
Typeset by Kelly Gray
Printed and bound by TJ International Ltd, Padstow, Cornwall

Learning Matters
33 Southernhay East
Exeter EX1 1NX
Tel: 01392 215560
info@learningmatters.co.uk
www.learningmatters.co.uk

FSC
Mixed Sources
Product group from well-managed
forests and other controlled sources

Cert no. SGS-COC-2482
www.fsc.org
© 1996 Forest Stewardship Council

Contents

Contributors

Jennifer Colloby

Jennifer Colloby has 14 years' experience of training and assessing students on ITT, STAC and most recently, EYP programmes at the Open University. She is currently the Course Chair of one of the Early Years Courses, Working with Children in the Early Years, and is a team member of the Open University's Early Years Foundation Degree. She has considerable experience of appointing tutors to a wide range of education courses as well as recruiting and training Assessors to work on the EYP programme.

Gill Goodliff

Gill Goodliff is a Lecturer in Early Years at the Open University where she teaches on work-based learning courses in the Sector-Endorsed Foundation Degree in Early Years and is a Lead Assessor for Early Years Professional Status. Her professional background with young children and their families was predominantly in the Public Voluntary and Independent sector. Her current research focuses on the professional development and identities of Early Years practitioners and young children's spirituality.

Lynn Trodd

Lyn Trodd is a Senior Lecturer in the School of Education at Hertfordshire. She has run the Phase 1 pilot for EYPS and is involved in teaching the National Professional Qualification in Integrated Centre Leadership, and the Sector-Endorsed Foundation Degrees in Playwork and in Early Years.

Zoe Raven

Zoe has been working in childcare since 1989, managing day nurseries, other childcare provision and a training centre in the Milton Keynes/Northants area. She has been an associate lecturer for the Open University on two of the Early Years Foundation Degree courses and has been assessing for the Early Years Professional Status since the original pilot scheme.

Jeanne Barczewska

Jeanne has been involved in childcare since 1988 running her own business for 12 years providing a range of childcare services including crèches, daycare and holiday clubs alongside consultancy and training. She was heavily involved in training and development within Northamptonshire working with the local authority and local FE colleges for a number of years. She has worked for two large provider groups as Quality and Development Manager over a period of 8 years. Jeanne is currently working for the Open

University as an Associate Lecturer on level 1 Early Years courses and for the University of Northampton as a lecturer on the Early Years Foundation Degree. Jeanne has been involved in EYPS since it began and also works as a freelance consultant.

Anna Corbett, Deputy Manager, Fenwood House Day Nursery

Margaret Dobbs, Principal, Cherrytrees Montessori Nursery School

Dawn Evans, Manager, Roundabout Christian Pre-School

Linda Fairlamb, Senior Staff Tutor, The Open University in the North

Ann Hume, Childcare Manager, North Lindsey College

Gillian Manasse, Senior Lecturer, Sheffield Hallam University

Mona Naqvi, Project co-ordinator for a family centre

Sarah Presswood, Nursery Manager, George Perkins Day Nursery

Alexandra Skvortsov, Proprietor, Greetland Private Day Nursery

Foreword from the series editors

This book is one of a series which will be of interest to all those following pathways towards achieving Early Years Professional Status (EYPS). This includes students on Sector-Endorsed Foundation Degree in Early Years programmes and undergraduate Early Childhood Studies degree courses as these awards are key routes towards EYPS.

The graduate EYP role was developed as a key strategy in government commitment to improve the quality of Early Years care and education in England, especially in the private, voluntary and independent sectors. Policy documents and legislation such as 'Every Child Matters: Change for Children' DfES (2004); the 'Ten Year Childcare Strategy: Choice for Parents – the Best Start for Children' HMT (2004), and the Childcare Act, 2006, identified the need for high-quality, well-trained and educated professionals to work with the youngest children. At the time of writing (June 2008), the Government's aim is to have Early Years Professionals (EYPs) in all Children's Centres by 2010 and in every full day care setting by 2015.

This book is distinctive in the series in that its particular focus is the assessment processes for the Validation Pathway towards achieving EYP Status. In The Validation Process for EYPS Jennifer Colloby gives a brief overview of the background to reform of the Early Years workforce. She explores the development of the graduate EYP role and discusses the importance of reflective Early Years practitioners who can lead practice and develop and support others in their roles. The book contains practical advice and suggestions for candidates as they prepare for each stage of the assessment process and is linked throughout to the National Standards for Early Years Professional Status.

Throughout the book EYPs working in different Early Years settings, and with a variety of job titles, reflect on and discuss their journey towards achieving EYPS to illustrate how candidates might approach each component of the process. These case studies and other reflective and practical tasks are used to deepen readers' understanding. Two experienced EYP assessors, Jeanne Barczewska and Zoe Raven, have written the detailed guidance to candidates for the final stages of the assessment process. The final chapter explores the imperative for continuing professional development beyond the achievement of Early Years Professional Status and examines new opportunities for career pathways.

The Validation Process for EYPS will support candidates on any of the pathways towards achieving Early Years Professional Status and we are delighted to commend it to you.

Gill Goodliff   Lyn Trodd

The Open University   University of Hertfordshire

June 2008

1 Setting the scene: the modern-day workforce

CHAPTER OBJECTIVES

By the end of this chapter you should:
- be aware of how the role of an EYP fits into the reform of the workforce;
- recognise the influences that have contributed to a changing workforce;
- have insight into the daily work of an EYP;
- be more aware of the opportunities that the EYP role will afford you.

This chapter considers the growth of the workforce and the creation of a new role, the Early Years Professional (EYP). It looks briefly at how the EYP role emerged as a result of government thinking, informed by a demand for the expansion in childcare and a need to meet a dynamic external environment. It considers the historical perspective that has led to a new, professionalised community of practitioners. It concludes with a case study from an EYP who reflects on the impact becoming an EYP has made on her role.

Introduction

There has never been a more exciting time for being an Early Years practitioner than now. The past ten years have witnessed a doubling in the number of childcare places to 1.28 million (Ofsted, 2007), thus demonstrating a significant shift within the childcare sector. The Secretary of State for Children, Schools and Families in his foreword to *The Children's Plan: Building Brighter Futures* (DCSF, 2007) sets out government plans that 'families will be at the centre of excellent integrated services' which will in part be realised through the expansion of Children's Centres across the country. With its commitment to 'ensure that every child has the best start in life' (DCSF, 2007) the government has identified that the most important factor for achieving this will be the development of a world-class workforce.

The Children's Workforce Development Council (CWDC) 'aims to improve the lives of children and young people by ensuring that the people working with children have the best possible training, qualifications, support and advice' (adapted from CWDC, 2006a).

Part of the overall reform of the children's workforce included plans to develop a new and pivotal role: that of the Early Years Professional (EYP). The aim is to have EYPs working in all Children's Centres offering childcare by 2010 and in every day care setting by 2015, and this will be facilitated through provision of training pathways to enable individuals to achieve EYP Status. These pathways include:

- the Validation Pathway for experienced graduate practitioners;

- a pathway for less experienced graduate practitioners who need targeted support to increase their underpinning knowledge and theory;

- a pathway for experienced practitioners who are studying to achieve graduate status; and lastly

- a training pathway for graduates from outside the workforce, to the role of EYP.

There now exist multiple opportunities for adults both within and outside the sector, to be part of this new Early Years workforce role, which has at its very heart the raising of standards and achievement in the care and education of young children. This does not mean that all that has gone before is now to be condemned as poor practice and disregarded; nor does it mean past achievements should be unrecognised. Rather, what was identified as best practice will be developed and expanded, and a fundamental role of an EYP will be to lead and model best practice amongst the communities of practitioners they work within.

There is now a commitment from government to fund the training and development of the Early Years workforce on a scale never seen before. This development (and demand) can in part be tracked back to events that often make uncomfortable reading; for example, the death of Victoria Climbié led directly to the revision of policy and practice reported in the Green Paper *Every Child Matters* (DfES, 2003). This crucial document has led to new policy initiatives designed to safeguard and improve outcomes for children. *Choice for Parents, the Best Start for Children: A Ten Year Strategy for Childcare* (HM Treasury, 2004) articulated the extent of the reforms to provision and the workforce. The CWDC was charged with the responsibility of allocating government funds, initially through the Transformation Fund, now the Graduate Leader Fund, to meet the demand for the training and development of a more highly qualified workforce.

You may be a long-standing practitioner who has witnessed the many policy changes impacting on practice over recent years, as well as the expansion of the Early Years workforce. You may be a graduate following the Full-training Pathway who finds yourself at the forefront of these new initiatives, or you may be a practitioner who has recently gained the necessary skills and experience to train for EYP Status. It is important to position yourself in the context of the radically changing workforce and to accept that in aspiring to be an EYP you are committed to change. By leading and supporting others you will, as part of a community of practitioners, help to make England 'the best place in the world for our children and young people to grow up' (DCSF, 2007).

A historical perspective of provision and the growth of the workforce

Over the past 100 years, provision has been the subject of considerable debate and change. The history of day care for young children can be most closely linked to the role of women and their access to paid work. The outbreak of the Second World War in 1939 led to a rapid expansion in the number of women entering the workforce. As a response to this, the then Ministry of Education introduced Nursery Centres for the care of babies and children of working mothers. The creation of these wartime Nursery Centres was politically motivated by a real need for an increased workforce and not out of any concern for the well-being of young children. Near the end of the war the 1944 Education Act included the continuation of 'nursery education', but, with finance short, many local education authorities (LEAs) were obliged to fund compulsory education for children from five years old rather than support non-statutory provision.

However, localised provision continued, with some LEA and privately funded day care together with part-time pre-school playgroups – often managed and run by groups of mothers – offering learning through play. By 1991 at least one year of funded education was available for those parents who wanted it, but overall provision was patchy and of variable quality. In 1994, the *Start Right* report (Ball, 1994) was published, in which Sir Christopher Ball outlined the case for government to review care and education, addressing the inequities of its provision across the country and making pre-school education a priority.

Since then significant developments in the sector have occurred. Clark and Waller (2007), record the following changes in early education and care:

- the increase in the quantity of provision;
- the relationship between care and education;
- the quality of provision;
- the appropriate curriculum for young children;
- the training of professionals.

(Clark and Waller, 2007, p.11)

The increase in provision can be traced back to the National Childcare Strategy (1997). Its intention was to link local authorities with the private and voluntary sector in order to extend and improve provision and increased opportunities for children. This resulted in the creation of Early Years Development and Childcare Partnerships (EYDCPs) within each local authority and a range of provision including statutory maintained nursery schools, privately funded crèches, childminders and nurseries as well as voluntary pre-schools and crèches. Extended (wrap-around) school care was introduced more recently as an initiative of *Every Child Matters* (DfES, 2003), which has set targets for all schools to meet this provision by 2010.

The integration of care and education also began in 1997 and continues today through the EYDCPs. A primary function of an EYDCP is to 'enhance the care, play and educational experience of young children by bringing together the maintained, private and voluntary sectors' (adapted from DfEE, 2001, p.3). The development and role of EYDCP in defining local services for families and young children are supported and complemented by the aims of the government's Sure Start initiative (2004). This initiative for tackling child poverty was to focus resources on those young children and babies considered to be disadvantaged and therefore to promote their physical, intellectual and social development in order to 'break the cycle of disadvantage for the current generation of young children' (Sure Start, 2004, p.2). The Children's Plan (DSCF, 2007) aims to build on the current entitlement of free early education and childcare and 'extend the offer of up to 15 hours of free early education and childcare to 20,000 2-year-olds in the most disadvantaged communities' (DCSF, 2007, p.9).

The regulation and inspection of the quality of provision is the responsibility of the Office for Standards in Education (Ofsted). As a result of the Childcare Act 2006 all provision must be both registered with Ofsted and, from September 2008, deliver the Early Years Foundation Stage (EYFS), which is the framework for the education and welfare of young children from birth to 5 years. In order to ensure a consistent approach to the inspection of the EYFS, Ofsted will align its Inspection Framework to the delivery of the EYFS whether in settings or schools. In addition, the trial by Ofsted of self-evaluation forms for settings was positive, and a revised self-evaluation form will now be included in the inspection of settings from September 2008.

Over recent years there have been significant developments in the integration of care and education. The Childcare Act 2006 introduces the EYFS, which is the first-ever legislative framework for Early Years and childcare. The EYFS aims to remove any distinction between learning and care, so reflecting an approach that the best practitioners have always taken. Building on previous developments in the curriculum,

> *The Foundation Stage (EYFS) brings together:* Curriculum Guidance for the Foundation Stage *(2000), the* Birth to Three Matters *(2002) framework and the* National Standards for Under 8s Daycare and Childminding *(2003), building a coherent and flexible approach to care and learning.*
>
> (DfES, 2007a)

The Childcare Act (2006) sets out the context for the delivery of the EYFS, and it is within this context that the role of the EYP makes such a significant contribution. EYPs will be responsible for leading and supporting their colleagues in the implementation of the EYFS. Their success in this role is crucial in ensuring that the settings and communities within which they work 'deliver the EYFS to an excellent standard' (DfES, 2007b, p.9). Chapter 3, Part 1 considers both the context that supports the delivery of the EYFS and how the role of the EYP is linked to the successful implementation of the EYFS.

CWDC is committed to creating a workforce that is well trained, supported and highly motivated. Drawing on the outcomes from *Every Child Matters* (DfES, 2003), it has ambitious plans to create a workforce of graduate and non-graduate staff with defined roles who by working together will raise the quality of provision for children and their families. The focus of this book is the newly created graduate role of the EYP. The EYP will need to demonstrate high-level skills and knowledge, as well as those skills which are crucial to leading and supporting others in their practice. *The Guidance to the Standards* (CWDC, 2007a) sets out the expectations for anyone wishing to achieve EYP Status and will be referred to throughout this book.

What follows is a case study written by an EYP. Dawn achieved EYP Status in February 2007 and in the case study gives an account of a day in her life as an EYP.

Meet one of today's Professionals

CASE STUDY

Dawn works as the EYP at Roundabout Christian Pre-School, a Church group with two settings, one offering full day care for 50 weeks a year and the other offering more traditional pre-school sessions during term time only. Dawn works at the full day care setting, and her role includes visiting the pre-school, supporting the work of the Supervisor and making sure the group's ethos is reflected in both settings. In this account she explains how achieving EYP Status has caused her to become a more reflective practitioner. She also acknowledges that, while the everyday issues that impact on how she leads and supports her staff have not gone away, she has now gained confidence to approach things differently in order to achieve better outcomes for children.

A day in the life of an Early Years Professional

As you would expect my day begins at home. I have three children of my own to sort out at the start of each day, two teenagers, and one young adult who is in the process of moving out and getting married. I'm usually the last in the bathroom so that I can tidy as I come out and again last in the kitchen for the same reason. On a good day I leave home at around 7.50 without having to answer the phone. More commonly at the moment and due to the current virus epidemic the phone rings with a message from a member of staff who is unable to come to work. This reminds me of the critical incident I had to write about as part of the written tasks, and one that has to be dealt with in my role of EYP.

First job on arrival at work is to check the rota and replace the member of staff if possible. We are lucky enough to be able to run with higher ratios than required by Ofsted. I consider that a ratio of 1:8 is not enough to enable staff to work with or observe small groups of children who are engaged in self-chosen activities, not to mention taking care of the toilet runs. We try and maintain a minimum ratio of 1:5. We are therefore able to work with one member of staff down in an emergency. A quick chat with the cleaner to make sure all is well and usual areas have been cleaned, the toilets are all in working order with the hand towels and soap changed. The Nursery Nurse is the next to arrive and she begins to clean the floor and baby bathroom. (The baby room is not cleaned by the church cleaner.) We catch up for a few minutes about the last evening shift and the expected day's events. One or two other staff members arrive before 8.30 and general routines begin, preparing the room or breakfast, particularly for the school-age children, as we offer wrap-around care. Part of the role of an EYP is being available to offer leadership and support to other staff, and I need to speak with the newer members of staff who need direction as to how the day will unfold. I wave to the school children leaving for school, checking their safety tabards and that they all have their school bags and that accompanying staff have the first aid bag and phone.

I try and settle at the computer, ensuring any cash or cheque payments for sessions handed over by parents are entered before the main session begins and between phone calls from parents. One of the most valuable outcomes from my EYP training was that I recognised the need to delegate some of my tasks. Therefore this was an area that I had tried to hand over to a bookkeeper. However, upon trial we realised this part of her role was not going to work out. Some of our children have similar first names, the same surname and parents have different names to the children. As the bookkeeper does not actually work with the children we had a few occasions when the payments were credited to the wrong family. Parents do not always return their invoices with payments, which would solve this problem. I had not realised how much information I was taking in when I entered the payments, subconsciously noting who had and had not paid and being able to chase parents as I chat to them. The bookkeeper is still responsible for entering the payments made through the bank, and I can keep an eye on these as I enter the other payments. As the bookkeeper becomes more used to parents and how they make their payments I hope we will be able to try again. However, we will have to find a way of communicating about unpaid accounts so that parents can be chased.

I have recently appointed a new member of staff to take over the under-3s in the main play room, and I have begun a handover process. The two staff members for the under-3s are working well together and I offer as much support as I can to them. I always make sure I speak with every member of staff, and sometimes this can be at lunch time if not in their room.

On going through the records the new Room Leader for the under-3s has reported unrecorded observations. This has caused me to reflect again on my role. I had presumed the previous member of staff had been keeping all necessary records up to date. A big lesson learned is that when delegating you need to reserve time for proper supervision, not just visual but also manual checking.

I digress slightly from a typical day but all these things need to be fitted in. As part of reflecting on my need to delegate, I had planned to find time to work alongside individual staff in a mentoring capacity as part of their and my own professional development. I feel strongly that all staff deserve to be supported and their practice developed, and I can do this by modelling my practice when working alongside them. Working alongside them will also help to foster an attitude of cooperation and collaboration. It would also give us the opportunity to reflect both on our practice and how we work with the children and others.

As sessions start and finish there are parents to chat to for various reasons, ranging from wanting to change sessions (this then involves checking the waiting list and changing sessions on the computer, then leaving messages for the bookkeeper to adjust invoices) to simply having a friendly chat about their life and their experiences. Parents like to know we care about them as well as the children.

With the impending introduction of the new Early Years Foundation Stage I need to plan for discussions and training sessions with other Room Leaders to make them aware of implications and changes to policy and procedure. I am confident that I know what needs to be done and that I will be able to cope. However, changing the paperwork is going to prove to be the greatest challenge. This will have to be discussed at the next Management Meeting to make the Committee aware of what needs to be done before the summer. When I am short-staffed I need to step in and cover, and this leaves me little time to address development needs during the day. Perhaps my working alongside the staff will have to go on hold for a short time as I know I will have to prioritise my time. In the past I would always put working with the children at the top of my list and that is why I studied for a degree. Taking paperwork home is something I am trying to stop.

The afternoon might include a visit from the local authority support team for a child requiring additional support. The key worker will need to be included/updated, as will the parents. Transition Meetings with local schools are currently happening once a half-term for children due to start school and will continue until July. As afternoon sessions draw to a close the 'After-School Pick-Up notebooks' have to be made up and any alterations to the normal register updated and checked by another Room Leader.

Two evenings a week I leave at 4pm and go home via the gym with my daughter. The other three evenings I work until 6.15pm supervising the After-School Club. Home for tea, relax in a bath for half an hour, then back to the computer to check e-mails or make any necessary adjustments to sessions or whatever has not been done during the day.

How has becoming an EYP made a difference to my day? It has made me reflect on my role and given me more confidence to stop trying to do everything myself. I have realised that, with proper support and supervision, trained staff can do the job as well as I can. I know that as an EYP I have to lead and support my staff and I am now much more confident in how I can do this and I set myself clear achievable targets to do this. My constant worry is staff shortage, but this I have to learn to manage and find ways of dealing with. The best bits of my day are the times when I can just play with the children, get totally engrossed with them and forget for a short time about the paperwork and usually the time. The children are worth the effort. They are why I am an EYP.

C H A P T E R   S U M M A R Y

You will from reading this chapter have gained insight into why provision is changing and how it is changing. The EYP role is clearly targeted to make a difference to the outcomes for children, and those who aspire to become EYPs must accept the challenges that this will bring. In the case study above, Dawn explains how she is aware of what needs to be done and reflects on how best she can achieve this. The government wants a high-quality, graduate-led profession of practitioners to implement its workforce reforms successfully. This is a time of change, of challenge and of commitment; it is about becoming an EYP.

Moving on

Chapter 2 explores the emerging role of the EYP and what it means to be a professional within the workforce.

Clark, M. M. and Waller T. (2007) *Early Childhood Education and Care Policy and Practice*. London: Sage

Pugh, G. and Duffy, B. (editors) (2006) *Contemporary Issues in the Early Years*, 4th edition. London: Sage

2 The role of the Early Years Professional

CHAPTER OBJECTIVES

By the end of this chapter you should have considered:
- what is meant by 'professional';
- the role of the EYP;
- the role of the EYP and the EYFS;
- the role of the EYP in leading and supporting colleagues.

Historically, certain groups of workers have always considered themselves to be 'professionals'. These groups, including doctors, lawyers and teachers, are usually self-governing, and the extended periods of training required by each of these groups of workers give them a specialised and valued body of knowledge that others do not have. Over recent years there has been an expansion in the number of occupational groups who consider themselves to have been 'professionalised'. Amongst these are practitioners working within the Early Years sector, and the creation of the role of the Early Years Professional has been welcomed by many in the Early Years workforce as an initiative offering recognition of their knowledge and expertise. This chapter explores what it is to be a 'professional' and what is expected of the role of the EYP.

Professionalism, reflective practice and the EYP

Professionalism is certainly not easy to define. Where we once collectively understood law, medicine and engineering to be the great 'professions', we now find that the word 'profession' is almost identical with that of occupation and the term 'professional' can be applied to sportsmen and women, hairdressers and actors. So what was once a term associated with high-status employment now crosses the boundaries into what once may have been described as craftsmanship. Professionalism or being a professional could possibly be defined as having attributes such as empathy and commitment that are of value and are attractive to the role. Early Years practitioners would consider that these values are an intrinsic part of their practice. There are also ways of behaving 'professionally', related to competence, knowledge and specific skills. Effective practice in Early Years requires practitioners to draw on specific skills. In addition, there are the numerous professional insights gained through experience and working alongside other colleagues. Teamwork and collaboration are part of the role of effective Early Years practitioners.

The characteristics, attributes or components of being a professional can also be extrapolated from the historically recognised professions. The common, fundamental characteristic of being a professional that emerges is that of being educated and trained. Avril Brock (2006) in exploring the dimensions of professionalism defines 'Education and Training' as being 'Higher Education, qualification, practical experience, obligation to engage in Continuing Professional Development'. When in 2006 CWDC created a new role within the Early Years workforce, that of the Early Years Professional (EYP), the features that characterised the long-standing professional roles could now be identified in this role. Early Years Professionals would be graduates, who by definition must have higher education experience. They would have leadership responsibilities from which they would draw on their practice with colleagues over an extended period of time. In addition CWDC expected that those who were drawn to the role of EYP would be 'committed, enthusiastic and reflective practitioners' (CWDC, 2007a, p.2), which acknowledges the many attributes and professional qualities that Early Years practitioners already had. CWDC were aware that within the Early Years workforce there were a significant number of graduates already working at 'EYP level' and able to achieve EYP Status quickly. However, in order to promote the growth of a professional Early Years workforce, CWDC created four training and assessment routes leading to the award of EYP Status. In addition to the Validation Pathway, which is the focus of this book, CWDC through its Full Training Pathway also seeks to attract graduates from other professions and with limited experience of working with young children. This means that in time the graduate-led Early Years workforce will have EYPs who, whilst sharing knowledge and understanding of theories of children's development and learning bring practical and professional skills (many seen as transferable skills) honed through degree-level study in other disciplines.

A reflective practitioner

The notion of being a reflective practitioner can now be considered central to a professional's effective practice. Paige-Smith *et al.* when discussing reflective practice describe how 'what is considered to be "good practice" and sound evidence for planning can be developed through reflection on practice' (2008, p.5). The exploration of a professional as someone who could 'think on their feet' was introduced by Donald Schön in his seminal book *The Reflective Practitioner* (1983). Schön's great contribution was to bring the concept of reflective practice to the heart of what professionals do. Reflective practice can simplistically be defined as 'reflection-in-action' and 'reflection-on-action'. Both require the professional to draw on previous experiences, consider the options available to them and create new understandings that inform their practice. This practice may involve the situation unfolding before you, requiring quick thought and action. This is what would be considered as reflection-in-action. This thinking on your feet or reflection-in-action is an immediate response to the presenting situation, in which you draw on past experiences to inform your immediate response. Later, in reviewing your action, by, for example, recording the incident, you engage in reflection-on-action. This reflective thought through which you spend time exploring all the factors that contributed to your action will in turn inform, refine and extend your future practice.

REFLECTIVE TASK

Think about two recent 'incidents' in your practice that caused you to 'think on your feet' and act. These could be described as 'critical incidents'. (You are required to submit a written task on a critical incident, and this is discussed in Chapter 6.) A critical incident is something that happened that was unforeseen and had to be dealt with immediately, such as an unexpected staff absence, a burst water pipe or an injury to a child or member of staff. Create a grid like that given in Table 2.1 to record your responses under each heading.

Table 2.1 Thinking about recent incidents

Brief notes on the nature of the recent incident	What action did you take?	What previous knowledge and experience informed your actions?	What, if anything, would you now do differently?	How has this incident informed your future practice?

Chapter 1 briefly outlined the significant changes to policy and procedure over recent years. In examining the response by the Early Years workforce to the implementation of new policies and procedures, Paige-Smith *et al.* found that 'inter-professional practices and the blended provision of integrated services are rapidly being introduced for young children' (2008, p.5). Changes to policy and procedure can be evidenced by, for example, the development and introduction of the Early Years Foundation Stage (DCSF, 2008a) that replaces the Curriculum Guidance for the Foundation Stage (QCA, 2000), the Birth to Three Matters framework (DfES, 2002) and the National Standards for Under 8s Daycare and Childminding (DfES, 2003). Integrated services can be found within the rapidly expanding number of Children's Centres as well as in other Early Years provision. Such services require professionals from multi-disciplinary backgrounds, to engage in professional collaboration in order to successfully implement policy. When examining policy change and its impact on the Early Years workforce, Brock supports the notion of a graduate-led Early Years workforce by suggesting that the Early Years sector 'requires an articulate, reflexive and highly qualified workforce, since the abilities to evaluate and develop policy and practices are key to its claims to professionalism' (2006, p.1). A professionalised workforce must therefore be able to explore, understand and evaluate policies and then develop the necessary practices through professional collaboration to support their implementation.

The concept of a graduate-led workforce is also supported by Paige-Smith et al., who contend that 'A key element in the development of inter-professional communities of practice for Early Years, is leadership of the team, by senior, reflective practitioners' (2008, p.6). A fundamental role of the EYP is the implementation of the Early Years Foundation Stage (DCSF, 2008a), the success of which is dependent on an EYP leading and supporting colleagues within a setting, and drawing on information and support from professionals in other disciplines. As inter-professional collaboration is now seen as crucial to policy implementation and its success, EYPs must therefore create the opportunities for this to happen. Teamworking and inter-professional practice are integral to the role of an EYP. Consider the group of Standards 'Teamwork and collaboration', Standards 33 to 36. Each of these four Standards demands that an EYP can work collaboratively and cooperatively with colleagues and other adults in ways that support children's development and learning (adapted from CWDC, 2007a, p.70). In Standard 33, EYPs must ensure they create a community of cooperation and support with colleagues, most particularly those in their own setting. This is what we would commonly define as team work or intra-professional practice. Standard 36 requires that an EYP can lead and support practice that contributes to the work of a multi-professional team. To do so requires the development of effective inter-professional practice, and this is a crucial role of an EYP.

Reflection

Sarah Presswood, who works as an EYP in a nursery in Birmingham, describes how inter-professional collaboration helped her lead and support her colleagues to develop further their inclusive practice when considering the needs of a young child who has hearing difficulties.

CASE STUDY

We have a little boy who has a severe hearing impairment attending nursery at the moment. The team supporting him comprises an educational psychologist, a speech and language therapist and a specialist teacher of the deaf. I felt it essential that, to support the little boy and to fully achieve an inclusive approach, we the staff should undertake some Makaton [signing] training. I worked with the speech and language therapist to devise an introductory training course for the staff. The therapist and I thought that it would be beneficial to invite the little boy's parents and other significant carers (e.g. grandmother and aunt) to the training so that he was being communicated with in a consistent manner. Since that initial training the therapist has been on hand with advice and follow-up input on any new signs that we might need.

It has been invaluable to be able to draw on the expertise of a specialist; we may know and understand what the boy is like better than the specialists who only see him for clinic appointments or occasional sessions but we could not address his particular needs without their expertise.

The role of the EYP is still in its infancy, and the subsequent development of communities of reflective practitioners has only just begun. The government is committed to the deployment of EYPs throughout all Children's Centres and day care settings. The creation of EYP networks within local authorities will be crucial to this deployment and to fostering greater understanding of the EYP role throughout the community. Chapter 8 considers this in more detail, together with a discussion of the opportunities for a professional voice for EYPs through the recently created Professional Association for EYPs.

Tensions may be experienced within a community, as inter-professional practice includes not only developing an understanding of other professionals' perspectives but also acknowledging and accepting differing ways of working. But by engaging with both intra- and inter-professional practice and reflecting on this practice, and by modelling good practice when leading and supporting colleagues, the role of the EYP will emerge as being of paramount importance to improving the quality of Early Years experience and so enable better outcomes for children.

Leadership and support: the role of an EYP

CWDC expects Early Years Professionals to be agents of change by improving practice in the settings in which they work. In order to bring about these improvements in practice CWDC attaches significant importance to leadership within the role of EYPs. The Gateway Review – the formative assessment tool in the Validation Process – requires all potential EYPs to demonstrate the necessary leadership skills. An acknowledged obstacle to managing or implementing change is a reluctance by some members of a community to accept change, whether in practice or in policy. Siraj-Blatchford and Manni identify an effective leader as 'one who recognises the inevitability of change and is able to plan for and manage change in such a way that those she leads are a part of the process' (2006, p.17). Ensuring colleagues feel part of any change process requires an effective leader to engage in both intra- and inter-professional practice, as discussed above. This will help colleagues to understand the purpose of change and should alleviate any tensions felt by them. Professional practice rooted in effective professional dialogue is supported by the Effective Provision of Pre-school Education Project (Sylva *et al.*, 2004), which found that better outcomes for children are directly related to the quality of their Early Years experience. They determined the characteristics of quality Early Years provision to include evidence of strong leadership developed through interactions with both colleagues and children.

In what ways can an EYP demonstrate leadership, manage change and create effective communities of practice? Siraj-Blatchford and Manni, when considering 'effective leadership in the Early Years', describe an effective leader as 'inspiring others with a vision of a better future' (2006, p.16). An effective leader must not only inspire the vision but also ensure that it is a collective vision within the community. This can be facilitated through the sharing of all objectives and working towards consistency in the practice of community members, and by engaging in both intra- and inter-professional practice. This can be achieved through engaging in both intra- and inter-professional practice. This not only ensures that all colleagues within the setting and wider community have a shared understanding of what the objectives are and which changes are to be implemented, but an EYP can draw on colleagues' strengths and expertise in order to achieve it. EYPs can work towards consistency in good practice within the setting and community by modelling good practice at all times. They can also help others to improve their practice by encouraging on-going professional development. Siraj-Blatchford and Manni also found that 'leaders of effective settings were both reflective in their own practice and encouraged reflection in their staff' (2006, p.18). Through the encouragement for and development of critical practice, EYPs will create a community of reflective practitioners who will share a vision of improved practice and consequently a commitment to embrace and implement change.

> ### REFLECTIVE TASK
>
> *Look back to the case study in Chapter 1 on page 5. Dawn discusses what she believes are the positive outcomes of intra-professional practice. What positive outcomes have been developed from your intra-professional collaboration? How do you ensure that these outcomes are shared by all your colleagues? How do you encourage and share critical reflection by and with your colleagues?*

Leadership and support

> ### PRACTICAL TASK
>
> *A visible role of an EYP is their leadership and support of colleagues. Look back to the short case study written by Sarah Presswood earlier in this chapter on page 12. In it there is clear evidence of her leadership and support of colleagues, evidence of teamworking and collaboration and evidence of partnerships with parents. Are you able to identify these? Can you link this evidence to the Standards? Now look back to the two critical incidents that you reflected on in the first reflective task on page 11. Choose one of them and make notes that clearly demonstrate:*
>
> * *your leadership and support of colleagues;*

- *knowledge you drew on to support your actions;*

- *any inter-professional support or multi-disciplinary working that informed your practice;*

- *identifying your practice against any of the Standards.*

Chapter 6 discusses the written tasks, one of which is a report of a critical incident. This task will be useful to you when thinking about and writing this report.

The next section considers the role of an EYP as she leads and supports colleagues towards the implementation of the EYFS.

The role of the EYP and the implementation of the Early Years Foundation Stage

The training and support of colleagues in the delivery of the EYFS is the fundamental role of an EYP. To be effective in this, EYPs must have a working knowledge of the EYFS and possess leadership skills that facilitate the leading and supporting of colleagues in its implementation. CWDC has identified three key skills that are seen as crucial for an EYP in being able to lead and support others in their practice. These three skills are assessed at Gateway Review and are as listed below:

- the ability to make decisions based on sound judgement;

- the ability to lead and support others;

- the ability to relate to, and communicate with, others.

(adapted from CWDC, 2007b, p.9)

Chapter 3, Part 1 considers the relationship between the role of the EYP as defined by the 39 Standards and successful implementation of the EYFS. The EYFS is further considered in Chapter 4 in terms of your knowledge of it as you prepare for final summative assessment. Preparation for Gateway Review is discussed in Chapter 5.

Below are three case studies written by Andra Skvortsov. Andra achieved EYP Status in February 2007 and is currently working as a manager of a day nursery with extended day care provision. Each of the case studies offers insight into Andra's role (as an EYP) on how she leads practice with colleagues who work with babies, toddlers and young children.

As you read each case study note the following.

REFLECTIVE TASK *continued*

- *how Andra draws on her own effective practice in order to lead and support her colleagues;*
- *how her role involves intra- and inter-professional collaboration;*
- *the types of evidence that can help to support demonstration of the EYP Standards.*

CASE STUDY

Leading and supporting colleagues in their practice with babies

Changing provision

I changed the emphasis of provision for children aged under 2, moving from focused activities to continuous provision. In my setting we define 'continuous provision' as the resources and activities that are always available to the children, whenever they choose to access them, as opposed to activities that are presented in specific time slots as defined by the practitioners. In this instance I wanted to change the provision so that the youngest children could have continual access to a wider range of activities than they had previously.

In line with the ethos of EYFS, which states that 'a rich and varied environment supports children's learning and development', I felt strongly that we needed to make changes in our provision for babies. Although some resources were available on a continuous basis, a lot of experiences were not available for children in this age group to choose according to their own interests, but instead were presented at fixed times as planned by the practitioners (Standards 1, 4, 7, 8, 9, 11, 13, 19).

To explore the issue further I held a meeting with the team leader for the under-2s and we brainstormed what exactly we felt high-quality continuous provision should look like and the barriers we thought we might face in achieving this. Following this meeting I planned a series of staff meetings to explore the topic of continuous provision with the practitioners working with the babies. I held monthly meetings for a period of five months during which we explored many different issues (Standards 33, 34, 35, 39).

At the first of these meetings we began by considering what young children are like, how they learn and what kind of environment they need to do this effectively. I provided a number of pictures of children in the age group 0–2 engaged in play as prompts, and this led on to a useful discussion which helped the practitioners identify key points of child development and their role in supporting this (Standards 2, 24, 37).

We then went on to examine the EYFS and considered the impact of the statements 'every child is a competent learner from birth' and 'Babies and children develop in individual ways and at varying rates. Every area of development – physical, cognitive, linguistic, spiritual, social and emotional – is equally important' (DCSF, 2008a, Principles into practice, 1.1). Through this discussion, practitioners were able to recognise that children need to play in different ways according to their own needs, and that our key role is in supporting that play, both through a well-resourced, accessible environment and through extending and supporting children's spontaneous play (Standards 8, 19). We agreed that very young children potentially learned little from adult-led activities and that sometimes it seemed that they participated in such activities to please us rather than because they enjoyed it.

I discussed with practitioners the concept that very young children need to use all of their senses if they are to learn and develop effectively and played them a short video of a child playing with glue. It was clear to them all that the child's main focus was not on creating an end product, but rather on the properties of the glue itself, how it felt, smelled and even tasted! This formed the basis of a discussion on how much time a child would need to fully engage in this kind of learning, and the conclusion that such learning could be severely hindered by the nursery 'routine' if we let it (Standards 10, 14, 21, 24, 33, 34, 35, 36).

We talked about the huge amount of different skills that young children need to develop: from physical skills such as sitting, crawling, walking and co-ordination skills, through categorisation, language and communication skills, and how we could support this development through the provision of carefully chosen resources and sensitive adult support (Standard 2). I directed the practitioners to the EYFS document and pointed out to them that one of its guiding principles is that 'the environment plays a key role in supporting and extending children's learning and development' (EYFS, Principles into practice card).

Finally we discussed the principle of continuous provision. We undertook a brief audit of our current provision and agreed that we could not truly describe an activity as 'continuous' if it was not available all of the time. Some practitioners expressed concerns over allowing such young children constant access to messier activities such as sand, water and paint, but we worked consistently over the next few months to gradually introduce these changes until we reached the point where all children have continuous access to items such as books, mark-making materials, paint, sand, water, dough, blocks, dressing up, musical instruments, puppets, dolls, toys and photograph albums, to name just a small selection. These items are made available for children during both indoor and outdoor play, and additional items are added according the particular interests of different children at different times (Standards 7, 8, 9, 11, 24).

CASE STUDY *continued*

Throughout this process I learned a great deal about how I could best manage change and the skills I needed to draw on to do so. Several practitioners were very keen to make lots of changes all at once and displayed a great deal of enthusiasm for the project, whereas some others were quite resistant and expressed the opinion that they didn't really agree with the changes. In my role as an EYP, I need to be an agent for change, so it was very important for me to find a way to help all the practitioners overcome their reluctance and embrace the change to their working practices. I learned that the process of change often has to be slower than I would like, and that it is important to take time to reflect on any changes as we implement them, as well as to explore all the issues that arise in order to move forward to the next stage (Standards 34, 35, 38, 39).

CASE STUDY

Leading and supporting colleagues who work with toddlers

I supported practitioners and parents in the transition of a 16-month-old girl with a very specific medical condition into nursery.

I first met H and her mother when I was approached by a parent about doing some fundraising for the charity that supports people with H's condition. As part of our fundraising we organised a 'sponsored sing', and to help the children understand why I invited H and her mother to spend some time in the nursery so that the children could meet H and learn about her condition. As a result of these visits H's mother approached me about the possibility of a place in the nursery for H. She explained that it was very difficult for H to build up social relationships with other children because of the risks associated with her condition, and she asked me if I thought the nursery would be able to help her.

I knew that I would need more information and possibly outside help to ensure that H was safe in nursery, so I planned a very slow transition with lots of visits.

The first thing I wanted to do was to find out more about H's condition. I looked it up in the CaF Directory of Specific Conditions and Rare Disorders (Contact a Family, London, 2002), and this led me to the website of the charity. As H's particular condition varies so much between individuals, the best source of information is usually the individual concerned, or in this case the parent. Because of this I had lots of informal chats with H's mum and asked her about the precise nature of the condition, what H could and couldn't do and what changes she thought the nursery would need to make to accommodate H. We had these chats in the room which H would be joining, and they formed part of her transition into nursery. Practitioners in the room were able to see how H and her mum interacted and I was able to model practitioner support for them (Standards 2, 3, 5, 13, 14, 18, 24, 29, 31, 32).

It was immediately clear that H would need constant one-to-one support in order to attend nursery, so I contacted the local inclusion consultant, whose role it is to advise schools and settings on matters relating to special educational needs and inclusion, to ask how we went about securing this (Standard 36). The process of securing funding for H's one-to-one support turned out to be much longer and more difficult than I anticipated. I worked closely with H's parents and acted as a liaison between them and the inclusion consultant to make sure that everyone had the information they needed to write their statements in support of H's needs (Standards 33, 34). The request for support was turned down the first time it went to panel, so we doubled our effort to get them to understand what a positive impact social interaction would have on H's life, not only immediately but for the whole of her future. On the second attempt the funding was granted.

I had identified a practitioner who would provide the one-to-one support for H and I facilitated meetings between her and H, and H's mum (Standards 13, 24, 34). I emphasised the vital role that H's mother had in providing us with all the information we needed to support H in the nursery environment. I ensured the practitioner had sufficient time to get to know the family well, and that she felt completely comfortable with her role before encouraging H's mum to begin to leave her at nursery for short periods of time. Gradually the time H was able to attend nursery increased until she was able to stay for a full session (Standard 36).

It was important that H was able to take part in every activity at nursery, and between her key person and her parents we were able to ensure that this happened. To help all the practitioners in the nursery to understand H's specific needs I arranged a full team training event involving H's mum and nurses who specialise in the condition. This gave all the practitioners in the nursery an understanding of H's needs and abilities and meant they felt more confident involving her in the nursery day (Standards 38, 39).

The final issue that arose was to raise the awareness of parents and children with regard to H's specific condition. Because her condition is exacerbated by physical contact, both H's mum and I agreed that it was vital that the other children understood that we must play gently with her. After discussing it with H's mum we agreed that I would write about H in the nursery newsletter to inform parents and that the practitioners would talk with the children in circle time or in their key groups (Standards 30, 32).

The main thing I learned from this process is how important it is to make sure that everyone involved gets clear and timely information. For example, all the nursery practitioners needed information about H's condition to help her to integrate into nursery, not just her support worker. I think if I was going through this process again I would ensure that the panel which makes the funding decisions had more detailed information from the outset about the educational and social benefits for H of starting nursery, to make it less likely that funding would be refused.

Leading and supporting colleagues who work with young children

The children's interest in countries around the world led to the introduction of language lessons in our pre-school room, which accommodates children from approximately 3 years old until they start reception class at school. The introduction of another language links with Communication, Language and Literacy in the EYFS, as it helps develop children's phonological awareness, listening skills and cultural knowledge (DCSF, 2008a, 4.4 EYFS card, Learning and Development, Communication, Language and Literacy).

In the course of a topic on summer holidays, several of the children in the pre-school room started to show an interest in different languages. The pre-school leader picked up on this and they began to incorporate a little bit of French into everyday activities, such as saying 'Thank you' and counting the cups at meal-times. When the children's interest increased as a result of this, the room leader approached me to discuss ways in which we could take it further, as she had already taught them the small amount of French that she knew (Standard 27).

Having discussed the situation with her, we agreed that it would be a good idea to approach a language teacher to come in and give the children a few lessons in basic French to see if we should take it any further. Following our meeting I contacted a local French teacher who was able to commit to a short lesson with the children once a week for approximately half a term. Because children attend our setting for a variety of different sessions we agreed that he would come on a Wednesday one week and a Thursday the next week, thereby ensuring that all the children were involved at least once every two weeks (Standards 11, 12, 15, 33, 35, 36).

The French lessons were a great success and the children successfully learned to say their names, count to ten and name some colours in French. Unfortunately the teacher was not able to commit to any further lessons so the pre-school leader and I discussed how we could keep the lessons going. She felt that the children benefited greatly from having someone coming in specifically to conduct a 20-minute language session so we agreed that I would take over that role. We also agreed that the children would benefit from a brief introduction to more than one language rather than a full year of French lessons, so we decided to offer a different language each term.

I approached the French teacher about giving me some guidance on how to teach a foreign language to young children, and he gave me lots of advice and helped me to plan some short 20-minute lessons involving lots of props, actions, singing and story telling. I then had another discussion with the pre-school leader and we agreed that I would teach a short class once a week and she and the other practitioners in the room would follow this up by singing the songs and reading the books that had been used in the lesson (Standards 36, 37, 38, 39).

CASE STUDY *continued*

Over the course of a few weeks we started to get very positive feedback from the parents, who were telling us that the children were singing their French counting song at home and telling their parents the names for the colours (Standard 32).

We have now moved on to a term of Spanish, and the children have completely settled into a routine of learning a new language. They know it is time for Spanish when I arrive in the room with my CD player and bag of props, and all say 'Hola!' as they sit down in the book corner ready for the lesson (Standards 15, 16, 25, 26, 27).

It has been very encouraging to see how enthusiastically the children have taken to this new challenge, and it has also raised lots of good opportunities to talk about different countries and cultures. During this time we have had a child with English as an additional language (EAL) start at the setting, and I think the experience of learning other languages has had a positive impact both on the children and on the practitioners in helping this child to adjust (Standards 12, 13).

I think the main thing I have learned from this experience is not to be afraid of trying something new. This is the first time I have attempted to 'teach' such young children by sitting them down as a whole group, and at first I was not at all sure as to whether it was appropriate or whether it would work. However, the children's enthusiasm and enjoyment speak for themselves and I think that, as long as such formal 'teaching' is a very small proportion of the time, it can be very effective (Standards 38, 39).

CHAPTER SUMMARY

Fom reading this chapter, you will have gained insight into the role of an EYP. Drawing on the historical aspect offered in Chapter 1, you explored what it means to be a professional. By looking at recent research into professionalism and considering this in relation to the role of an experienced Early Years practitioner you can understand more fully the pivotal role an EYP will play in the changing environment of the Early Years sector. By accepting that the concept of being a reflective practitioner is intrinsic to being considered a 'professional', you considered how this impacts on intra-professional and inter-professional practice. These are explored again in terms of your continuing professional development in Chapter 8. The three case studies offered a perspective into how an EYP leads and supports her colleagues across the three age ranges. Additionally they detail how the EYP was implementing the Early Years Foundation Stage and how through the discussion she evidenced she met the relevant EYP Standards.

Moving on

In Chapter 3 you will look more closely at the Standards which must be met to achieve EYP Status. Part 1 of Chapter 3 looks at the link between the Standards and the role of an EYP and their impact on the key issues for implementing the Early Years Foundation Stage. Part 2 of Chapter 3 provides a complementary approach to understanding selected Standards.

FURTHER READING

Penn, H. (2005) *Understanding Early Childhood: Issues and Controversies*. Maidenhead: Open University Press

Chapter 6 – 'Past, Present and Future' – looks at the history of childhood and the development of policy making for young children in the UK

Miller, L. and Cable, C. (editors) (2008) Professionalism in the Early Years. London: Hodder Arnold.

Chapter 11 Moss, P. (2008) 'The Democratic and Reflective Professional: Rethinking and Reforming The Early Years Workforce'. This is a challenging chapter examining the changes in early childhood care and education in Britain. The author argues for a rethink of the values underpinning policy and workforce reform together with a call for greater recognition of the professional role of workers and improvements to pay and employment.

3 The Standards

This chapter is divided into two parts. Part 1 considers how the role of the Early Years Professional (EYP) can be identified within the context that has been created to support the delivery of the Early Years Foundation Stage (EYFS). It considers how the Standards that define the role of an EYP impact on the successful implementation of the EYFS. Part 2 considers five of the Standards and offers examples of how you can identify evidence of your practice. Both parts assume that you have a developing working knowledge of the Standards.

PART 1

Introduction

This chapter could simply list the 39 Standards and offer explanation and advice to understanding and achieving them. However, that could lead to a 'can do' approach, reducing the Standards to a set of skills not worthy of the role of a graduate aspiring to achieve EYP Status. Instead it seeks to build on the discussion in Chapters 1 and 2, where the emerging role of an EYP, its focus on engaging with reflective practice and its place within a professionalised workforce were considered. This approach is supported by CWDC, which, in the *Guidance to the Standards*, advises that:

> It is necessary to consider the Standards as a whole to appreciate the skill, creativity, commitment, energy and enthusiasm required for leading practice in the early years and the intellectual and leadership skills required to be an effective EYP.

> (CWDC, 2007a, p.5)

Professional insights, or ways of behaving professionally, as well as a wealth of prior experience, will impact on your interpretation of the role of an EYP, making the role a unique one to you. This uniqueness is supported by the flexibility of the assessment in order to achieve EYP Status, which allows for 'different ways in which candidates in different settings can provide evidence that they are meeting the standards' (CWDC, 2007a, p.5). This means, for example, that if you work in a small setting with just two or three colleagues you will be directly involved with policy writing, and you will need to demonstrate how you involve your colleagues in the creation of a policy. By contrast, if you work in a larger setting or in a setting that is part of a group, you may not be responsible for policy writing. In this instance you will have to demonstrate how you feed into policy writing by, for example, offering to pilot a new initiative and then evaluating it.

To achieve Early Years Professional Status and become an EYP 'candidates are required to demonstrate they meet all the standards laid out in this document' (CWDC, 2007a, p.3). The Standards are organised into six groups and reflect the expectations of a professional role that embraces the following:

- knowledge and understanding;
- effective practice;
- relationships with children;
- communicating and working in partnership with families and carers;
- teamwork and collaboration;
- professional development.

(CWDC, 2007a, p.3)

In order to achieve EYP Status, all 39 Standards have to be met. You will need to draw on evidence from your practice with babies, toddlers and young children and be able to offer it in support to meet the requirements of each of the Standards. You must demonstrate that your practice is both relevant to the role of an EYP and current. You are allowed to draw on practice from the past three years at the point of registration on the Validation Pathway. It is vital that your evidence demonstrates clearly that you have been in a role of leading and supporting others to facilitate the development of their practice. The case studies in Chapter 2 illustrated ways in which Andra led and supported the work of others when working with babies, toddlers and young children.

You also need to understand that the Standards do not work in isolation (the 'can do' approach) but that they intertwine and both relate to and impact on each other. For example, Standards 1–6 inform all aspects of 'effective practice', group 2 of the Standards. In the following brief account, drawn from an exemplar used at assessor training, links between the Standards can be clearly identified:

CASE STUDY

Jane reorganised methods of observation for babies, toddlers and young children which would then be used to inform planning. This shows an example of drawing on good practice from the EYFS, Standard 1. At the same time it requires Jane to lead and support others in the implementation of new observation techniques – Standard 34. An outcome is that this addresses the EYFS practice requirement underpinning the principles of 'A Unique Child' and 'Enabling Environments' and thus supports effective practice for meeting the requirements of Standard 10 ('Use close informed observations . . .') and Standard 13 ('Make effective personalised provision . . .').

In the following reflective task you will think about your own practice in leading practice in the EYFS.

PRACTICAL TASK

A simple method for considering how Standards link to and impact on each other within your practice may be facilitated by the following task. First, reflect on or think of an approach that you have drawn on from the EYFS. Record the ways in which you led and supported others to implement the activity or experience. Then finally evaluate its outcomes in three ways.

- *How has it improved the outcomes for the children, and what Standards does this meet?*

- *How has it developed the work of others, and what Standards does this meet?*

- *What have I learned and what would I do differently?*

Part 2 of this chapter explores this theme further by considering five Standards in more detail.

The EYP and the EYFS

Through the introduction of the EYFS in September 2008, EYPs will ideally act as change agents to improve practice and will 'be expected to lead practice across the EYFS in a range of settings, modelling the skills and behaviours that promote good outcomes for children and supporting other practitioners' (adapted from CWDC, 2007a, p.4). Chapters 1 and 2 considered the role of the EYP and offered insight into how an EYP can lead and support the work of other practitioners. The EYFS has set Standards so that Early Years providers can emulate the kind of personalised provision that parents offer to their children at home. These Standards state that providers should deliver individualised learning 'that enhances the development of children in their care and gives those children the best possible start in life' (DfES, 2007a). Throughout the *Statutory Framework for the Early Years Foundation Stage* (DCSF, 2008c), the necessity for practitioners to engage both with parents and with other professionals is emphasised, as this is seen as essential to improving the outcomes for all children. To create an effective framework for partnership working, practitioners must share relevant information with each other about children who may receive education and care in multiple settings. They must develop close working links with parents to ensure they can identify learning needs and offer support to extend this learning within the child's home. They must further engage with professionals from other agencies to both identify and meet the needs of children. To achieve successful implementation of the EYFS, requires EYPs both to recognise the context they work within that supports the delivery of the EYFS and to ensure the delivery of the key issues of the EYFS that have been highlighted.

The professional context is extensive, as it draws upon all partners within a local authority to work together to raise the standards in Early Years care and education provision. Such a multi-disciplinary approach, bringing together partnership working with parents as well as professionals in health, education and social care, will require the development of inter-professional practice in order to best support effective delivery of Early Years education and care for children. As discussed in Chapter 2, an EYP will need to create, develop and build on inter-professional practice; and much of this part of the role is defined by Standards 29 to 36. Look back now to Chapter 2, where Sarah Presswood describes how through inter-professional collaboration she was able to offer a more inclusive approach to a young boy with hearing difficulties.

The importance of developing good working relationships with parents, not just to impart information to them but to draw on their understanding of their child's needs, requires a sensitive approach. Standards 29–32 are concerned with how an EYP should communicate and work in partnership with parents and carers. In particular, Standard 29 requires an EYP to demonstrate that they 'recognise and respect the influential and enduring contribution that families and parents/carers can make to children's development, well-being and learning' (CWDC, 2007a). The crucial role that parents play in children's development is now recognised, and the reflective task below expands on how you can develop your partnership with parents by drawing on inter-professional collaboration with colleagues.

REFLECTIVE TASK

Developing partnerships with parents

Every Parent Matters (DfES, 2007b) explains why partnerships with parents are important and suggests ways to develop them. The development of multi-disciplinary working or integrated services requires professionals to 'signpost' to parents what services are available within the community in addition to those within their own setting. Creating the 'signposting' will need professionals to collaborate and work together.

Consider the services currently provided within your setting as well as those that you signpost parents to in your locality. Indicate other professionals involved in providing these services. Table 3.1 on page 27 will support you in this task, and an example is given to you.

Table 3.1 Identifying multi-disciplinary working

Type of service available	Name	Which other professionals are involved	Engaging with this gives evidence of Standards
Parents who have multiple births	TAMBA – the Twins and Multiple Birth Association	Health visitor	S29, S31, S36

The over-arching aim of the EYFS is to ensure that every child achieves the five outcomes that arose from *Every Child Matters* (DfES, 2003), and it adopts a principled approach in order to do so. The principles are grouped into four distinct themes which describe how practitioners can support the development, learning and care of young children. The *Practice Guidance for the Early Years Foundation Stage* (DCSF, 2008b) illustrates how best this can be done and offers *Principles into Practice* cards which support practitioners in their work. In Chapter 2 Andra referenced her use of the principles into practice cards in a Case study, and you may find it helpful to look back at this on page 17.

The *Practice Guidance* also identifies the key issues (DCSF, 2008b, p.6, para.1.6) which are considered to be of paramount importance to the successful implementation of the EYFS and therefore to meeting the needs of all children. The key issues for implementation of the EYFS and the role of the EYP must be mutually dependent. It therefore follows that the Standards that define the role of an EYP must match the requirements for successful implementation of the EYFS.

The *Practice Guidance* identifies that one of the key indicators of a high-quality, continuously improving setting will be that it provides 'sustained shared thinking' – an awareness that adults working with children will support and extend children's thinking through involvement in shared tasks and experiences (DCSF, 2008b, p. 9). Standard 16 requires that an EYP must 'engage in sustained shared thinking with children' (CWDC, 2007a, p.8). The amplification for this Standard goes on to describe how an EYP must plan and provide for opportunities for this and encourage and support colleagues in engaging with this kind of interaction with children. The EPPE research (Sylva *et al.*, 2004) identified the provision of 'sustained shared thinking' as influencing high-quality provision for Early Years. You considered this influential aspect within the role of an EYP both in the case study in Chapter 1 and when considering intra- and inter-professional practice in Chapter 2. This clearly demonstrates the interdependent relationship between what makes for successful implementation of the EYFS and how the role of the EYP is defined by a Standard or Standards. It further demonstrates that the EYFS has been developed out of rigorous research on what defines best practice and confirms the importance of the graduate role of an EYP in leading effective practice to improve outcomes for children. There are many more examples of how the role of the EYP can link to the key issues highlighted in the *Practice Guidance for the Early Years Foundation Stage*. Table 3.2, which is part of the reflective task, is not exhaustive but further demonstrates the co-dependency between successful implementation of the EYFS framework and the EYP role.

REFLECTIVE TASK

Table 3.2 identifies key issues for successful implementation of the EYFS (column 1), and in column 2 identifies some of the Standards which relate to this.

1. *By considering the key issues that are listed and drawing on Guidance to the Standards, see how many more Standards can be matched to the key issues.*

2. *A third column has been added for you to identify evidence within your practice against the Standards and hence support implementation of the key issues. An example has been done for you.*

3. *Try to find three examples of your practice for each of the key issues. This will help you both in preparing for your written tasks and in identifying supporting evidence, which is covered in Chapter 6.*

Table 3.2 Implementation of the EYFS and the role of the EYP

Key issues for successful delivery	Identification of Standards within the role of an EYP	How I have done this in my practice
Meeting the diverse needs of children: through personalised learning, promoting positive attitudes to diversity, planning for the needs of children from ethnic minority backgrounds and planning for each child's individual care and learning requirements	2, 12, 28, 34	I have delivered training to staff on the Common Assessment Framework.

Partnership working: with parents and other professionals	6, 29, 30, 31, 36
Flexible provision: ensure effective continuity for children who attend more than one setting; differing needs of children	14, 36
Play: opportunities for indoor and outdoor play; well-planned opportunities for play; the role of the practitioner in play	12
Quality improvement: to create, maintain and improve a setting; a safe, stimulating environment; well-qualified staff; effective practice and professional development; effective challenge; sustained shared thinking; monitoring information and data	The group of standards on effective practice 38

Moving on

Part 2 of this chapter will now look at five Standards in greater detail. It will draw on your working knowledge of the Standards and expand on aspects of leadership and support as well as partnerships with parents and other professionals.

PART 2

Exploring your knowledge of the Standards

The role of the EYP is defined by 39 Standards, and to achieve EYP Status it is essential that the requirements to meet the Standards are understood. An essential aspect of understanding the breadth and depth of the Standards is often overlooked by candidates. This is the amplification to each Standard provided immediately below each Standard in the *Guidance to the Standards* (CWDC, 2007a).

In *Guidance to the Standards* and the amplification of each Standard, the essential characteristics of Early Years practice are identified by the use of 'must' or 'should' or 'will'. For example, Standard 7 states that 'Candidates must demonstrate their commitment to raising the achievement of all children . . .' and goes on further to state that 'Candidates should demonstrate they meet this Standard in every aspect of their planning . . .') (CWDC, 2007a). Alternatively, the use of 'might' or 'may' offers the candidate the opportunity of exploring alternative ways of evidencing the Standard. For example, Standard 7 explains that 'Candidates' leadership and support of others may be evidenced in several ways' (CWDC, 2007a). The 'may' allows for differing approaches to leadership and support to be offered by candidates and so allows for each EYP to operate in a way that is unique to them. Think back to Part 1 of this chapter, which considered the different ways that candidates in small and large settings have opportunities to be involved in policy writing.

This section looks now in more detail at Standards 11, 18, 21, 33 and 39. It draws partly on the work of Gillian Manasse, who has supported candidates training to achieve EYP Status. It offers the five Standards in a slightly different format, though the wording and content are identical to that in the current edition of the *Guidance to the Standards*. This different format should enable you to identify and highlight the specific detail which is expected in order to demonstrate achievement of each Standard:

- in your own practice; and

- in your leadership and support of others.

This alternative approach is meant to be supportive and complementary to your reading of *Guidance to the Standards*. As you read the five Standards below you may also want to refer to the relevant pages in the *Guidance to the Standards*. At the end of the section there is a reflective task that will help you identify your own practice and your leadership and support of others.

Standard 11

Plan and provide appropriate child-led and adult-initiated experiences, activities and play opportunities in indoor, outdoor and in out-of-setting contexts, which enable children to develop and learn.

To meet this Standard, candidates must demonstrate that they plan and provide experiences that have the following main characteristics:

- *First, they should be planned and purposeful, and give children opportunities to develop and learn.*

- *Second, they should be relevant, with content that matches children's ages, needs, interests and learning styles.*

- *Third, they should be developmentally appropriate for the different starting points from which children develop their learning and that build on what they can already do.*

- *Fourth, they should be sustained in that they give children time to become engrossed, to work in depth and to complete activities; and,*

- *Fifth, they should be comprehensive in that they cover all areas/aspects of the new Early Years Foundation Stage and help children to achieve the outcomes within* Every

Child Matters. *Overall, the experiences should be child-oriented in that they enable children to become competent learners.*

Candidates should lead and support others in providing activities that are planned and initiated by both adults and children.

- *Their leadership may be evident in the way they promote, with colleagues, the importance of safe, indoor and outdoor play settings for promoting children's well-being, development and learning.*

- *It may be evident in the encouragement they provide for their staff to stimulate and inspire children, to foster their independence, motivate them and promote their personal and social development.*

- *It may be evident in the way that the staff undertake risk assessments and take all reasonable precautions without restricting opportunities for children.*

Standard 18

Promote children's rights, equality, inclusion and anti-discriminatory practice in all aspects of their practice.

Candidates must demonstrate that:

- *They plan to meet the needs of all children, promote and uphold children's rights and that they actively promote equality of opportunity and anti-discriminatory practice.*

- *They will ensure that no child is excluded or disadvantaged because of ethnicity, culture or religion, home language, family background, special educational needs, disability, gender or ability.*

- *Whether or not there is a diverse population in the candidate's setting, candidates should show that they promote positive attitudes to diversity and difference with children and adults: for example, by helping children to learn about and value different aspects of people's lives.*

- *They should encourage children to acquire an appreciation of and respect for their own and other cultures in a way that promotes tolerance and harmony with other cultures and traditions.*

Some children from minority ethnic groups or with special educational needs and/or disabilities may experience discrimination and barriers to participation and learning. Candidates should show how they target support to remove barriers, where these exist, and to include such children fully in all aspects of provision.

- *For example, for children learning English as an additional language, this may involve building on children's experiences of language at home and in the wider community by providing a range of opportunities to use their home language(s), so that their developing use of English and other languages support one another.*

- *For children with special educational needs and/or disabilities, this may involve planning for their inclusion in all activities through providing additional support from adults, adapting activities or environments, providing alternative activities, or using specialist aids and equipment.*

- *Candidates will protect children's rights, in the context of Every Child Matters and anti-discriminatory legislation. Given social inequalities, they will provide a safe and supportive learning environment, free from harassment, in which the contribution of all children is valued and where racial, religious, disability and gender stereotypes and expressions of discrimination or prejudice are consistently challenged.*

- *They will be able to monitor and evaluate provision and practice in order to identify and remove any discrimination.*

Candidates should show how they lead and support colleagues to promote children's rights, equality and inclusion.

- *For example, some candidates may be able to show that, when children's rights have been infringed, such as in matters of safeguarding, they have advised colleagues about when and how they should act themselves, and when and to whom matters should be referred.*

- *Some may have evidence of working with colleagues and professionals from other agencies to remove barriers to learning and development;*

- *Whilst others may have led team discussions on the nature and avoidance of stereotypes and discrimination.*

Standard 21

Assess, record and report on progress in children's development and learning and use this as a basis for differentiating provision.

Candidates must be able to:

- *Apply their knowledge and understanding of the Early Learning Goals to determine children's progress towards them.*

- *They should be able to use information from systematic and routine observations to promote, record and track children's progress towards these goals. This is the basis for differentiated and personalised provision.*

Candidates must be able to:

- *Comply with the assessment and reporting requirements of the Early Years Foundation Stage.*

This means that they can:

- *Complete the Early Years Foundation Stage Profile;*

- *Summarise the information it contains and use it as the basis of clear oral and/or written reports to parents/carers on children's general progress and achievements; and,*

- At the end of the Early Years Foundation Stage, provide information for teachers in Key Stage 1 to ensure a smooth transition from the setting to school.

Candidates should be able to manage the assessment process so that the progress of all children in respect of all the Early Learning Goals is kept current by arrangements for:

- the observation of children,

- procedures for the recording and dissemination of information, and

- arrangements to ensure that the information derived from assessment will be used to inform future practice and provision.

Candidates should be aware that some children may have additional needs and might, therefore, benefit from additional assessment so that practitioners can better support their development and learning.

Candidates should demonstrate that:

- They understand the Common Assessment Framework (CAF), know how to complete it and understand how CAF core data can help professionals from all agencies work together to identify and address any factors from outside the setting that may be affecting a child's learning and development.

Candidates' leadership of practice might be demonstrated in several ways:

- For example, briefing colleagues about key assessment objectives, and how evidence to support the assessment should be gathered, recorded and reported.

- They might encourage colleagues to contribute assessment evidence in planning and evaluation meetings to back up views on next steps or for modifying or improving practice.

- Or they might train colleagues in how to complete the Early Years Foundation Stage Profile, the Common Assessment Framework and any other assessment schedules used in the setting.

Standard 33

Establish and sustain a culture of collaborative and cooperative working between colleagues.

To meet this Standard, candidates should demonstrate that they:

- work collaboratively and cooperatively with colleagues and other adults to enhance children's welfare, development and learning, and

- deploy colleagues who work directly to them or under their supervision in ways that support children's development and learning.

They will lead practice and plan, manage and direct the work of colleagues who work directly to them or under their supervision.

- At the same time, candidates will work in partnership with colleagues to plan, deliver, evaluate and improve practice and provision.

- They will involve colleagues in monitoring, assessment and record keeping.

Candidates will draw upon the knowledge and skills of colleagues and encourage them to share expertise through, for example,

- mentoring,

- shadowing,

- coaching.

Standard 39

Take a creative and constructively critical approach towards innovation, and adapt practice if benefits and improvements are identified.

Early Years Professionals should work continually to evaluate and improve practice and provision to achieve the best possible outcomes for children.

As part of their role, they may be required to consider using new or existing products or services, improving practices, procedures, systems and ways of working, either within or outside the setting.

To meet this Standard, candidates must demonstrate that:

- They can think creatively and are open to innovative suggestions from others and that they encourage colleagues to put forward their ideas.

- Further, they should provide opportunities for new ideas to be considered by colleagues and, where appropriate, selected for further development, and encourage colleagues to take acceptable risks in pursuing innovation and to make and learn from their mistakes.

They will discuss and agree ways in which selected innovations can be implemented and evaluated, and ensure that colleagues who originated or developed any ideas that are successfully implemented receive recognition for their achievement.

Candidates' leadership and support may be demonstrated by:

- Suggesting, piloting and evaluating innovations.

- They may directly support colleagues' implementation of new ideas, monitor and review progress with them, and subsequently help them to integrate successful innovations into everyday practice.

From reading the five Standards above and thinking about both your own practice and your leadership and support of others, you will be aware that, when considering the 39 Standards, there is a lot of evidence to provide. This evidence will cover a range of skills for each Standard, and it is important to note that this will be drawn from a variety of areas within your role. These areas, such as your role with colleagues in the setting, partnerships with parents and inter-professional practice, have all been considered in Chapters 1 and 2. As you prepare for assessment, most particularly for your written tasks and the tour (see Chapter 6), you need to reflect on how best the different facets of your role and responsibilities might enable you to demonstrate each Standard. You also need to consider the types of evidence that will support this. The different types of evidence, such as 'face-to-face' evidence, documented evidence and environmental evidence, must all relate directly to your own role within the setting. Face-to-face evidence will be drawn from your direct contact with colleagues, parents and children. Documented evidence will support face-to-face evidence and can be minutes of meetings, reports, policies, etc. Environmental evidence will be drawn from the direct impact you have made on your setting; for example changes to how information is made available to parents and visitors, creating more open-plan areas, etc. The following reflective task supports you in recognising the three types of evidence from your practice. It is suggested that you use the five Standards discussed above to do this, but you may wish to use other Standards instead. A suggested approach could be to do the task first with a Standard you are confident about and then repeat it for those you are less confident about. This will help you identify any gaps in the types of evidence you need to support your practice but is not necessarily indicative of areas of weakness in your practice. You may find your EYP Standards Self-Review Notepad useful to draw on.

PRACTICAL TASK

Table 3.3 lists the two characteristics of Standard 39 as described above. It then gives a brief explanation of identified evidence from a candidate's own practice and in the role of leading and supporting others.

Create your own tables for the task below and for the five Standards that are listed above: 11, 18, 21, 33, 39.

REFLECTIVE TASK

You can now look back at the tables you have created and identify where your evidence can be used for other Standards. For example, in Table 3.3:

- *the open afternoon for Parents will help demonstrate Standards 31 and 32;*

- *the initial meeting with the Health Visitor will help demonstrate Standard 36.*

Record these other Standards in your table or make notes underneath similar to the bullet points listed. Working within and between the Standards in such a fashion will help you develop your working knowledge of them and facilitate finding evidence from your practice.

Table 3.3 *Identification of practice for Standard 39*

Characteristic of Standard	Practice: face to face	Practice: documented	Practice: environmental	Leadership and support: face to face	Leadership and support: documented	Leadership and support: environmental
Think creatively, open to suggestion	At a staff meeting (Nov) suggested we needed to improve sun screening	Wrote to LA asking if funding available for canopy/ sunscreen	Risk assessment on outdoor area: did not provide enough shade	Discussed with Tricia what improvements she had thought of	Arranged for Tricia to visit two settings to look at outdoor area	Agreed ideas with Tricia on how she could improve the outside area
Provide opportunities for new ideas by colleagues	Tricia volunteered to attend seminars organised by Health Visitor	Leaflets and notes from initial meeting with the Health Visitor	Put a suggestion board in entrance lobby for staff/ parents/visitors	Supported Tricia's input at staff meeting (March) regarding sunscreen and shade	Agreed to letter from Tricia to parents asking for volunteers	Supported Tricia when she hosted an open afternoon for parents on Sun Safe

C H A P T E R   S U M M A R Y

Gaining insight into the Standards requires you to reflect on all aspects of your practice and then match it to the 39 Standards. In addition you need to be able to provide evidence to support all aspects of your role. You have considered how the role of an EYP helps to meet the key issues for implementing the EYFS. You have thought about the facets of your role and the different types of evidence you need to draw on to meet the Standards. The chapter has suggested reflective tasks to enable you to start the process of identifying the facets of your role within the Standards and the types of evidence to support your role, as you work towards achieving EYP Status.

Moving on

This preparation will feed into Chapter 6, which explores in greater depth how you can identify and draw on evidence in preparation for the written tasks and the setting visit. In Chapter 4 you will read about the assessment process in more detail.

FURTHER READING

DCSF (2008) Building Brighter Futures: next steps for the Children's Workforce. http://www.dfes.gov.uk/publications/childrensplan/downloads/7482-DCSF-WorkforceMatters.pdf

Early Years Foundation Stage. www.standards.dcsf.gov.uk/eyfs/

Goldschmeid, E. and Jackson, S. (2004) *People Under Three: Young Children in Day Care*, 2nd edition. London: Routledge

Hallet, E. (2004) 'The Reflective Practitioner', chapter 2 in Macleod-Brudenell, I. [ed.] *Advanced Care and Education Level 4 and 5*. Oxford: Heinemann Educational

For intra and inter-professional working in the Early Years:

Willan, J., Parker-Rees R. and Savage J. (editors) (2007) *Early Childhood Studies*, 2nd edition. Exeter: Learning Matters

Chapter 14 Working with Colleagues by Caroline Leeson and Valerie Huggins

4 Assessment overview and identifying preparatory support

CHAPTER OBJECTIVES

By the end of this chapter you should:
- understand the components of the assessment process;
- know how to prepare yourself for assessment;
- understand the role of the assessor;
- have critically reflected on the required knowledge and skills to demonstrate achievement of the Standards for EYP Status and begun to identify good supporting evidence to meet the Standards and groups of Standards.

This chapter outlines the components of the Validation Pathway. The characteristics of each component are briefly discussed and signpost you to other chapters in the book which address them in more detail. In this chapter you are provided with an approach to your preparation. The reflective tasks and case study material aim to help you to start to analyse your knowledge and practice in preparation for all the components and to identify what support you might draw on to do so.

Overview of the assessment structure

In order to gain EYP Status all candidates are required to undertake the components that make up the Validation Pathway. Those candidates who take the Validation Pathway only are expected to have 'considerable knowledge, experience and skills relative to the EYP Standards' (CWDC, 2007b, p.5) and as such are expected to be working at EYP level or to be very close to meeting the Standards required to be an EYP. The Children's Workforce Development Council has developed three other pathways to support those who wish to become EYPs, and the components of the Validation Pathway are included within them.

The Validation Pathway is in two parts. The first part is when you undertake Gateway Review, which is based on the assessment of three key skills that are deemed necessary for an EYP both to be an effective practitioner and to lead and support others to improve their practice. Prior to Gateway Review you will also have to prepare and submit a

Standards reflection to your provider. This is explained below. All aspects of the Gateway Review are fully discussed in Chapter 5.

If successful at Gateway Review you will move on to the second part of the Validation Pathway, when you will undertake final summative assessment leading to award of EYP Status. Final summative assessment is twofold. First, you will need to prepare and submit seven written tasks in which you analyse and discuss your practice against the 39 Standards. This is cross-referenced to a file of supporting documentary evidence drawn from your practice to help in achievement of the Standards.

The second part is the setting visit – a visit by an assessor to your setting during which the assessor seeks confirmation of the evidence you have claimed within the written tasks and looks for evidence of you demonstrating the wider role of the EYP. The written tasks and identifying supporting evidence are considered in Chapter 6. The setting visit is covered in Chapter 7.

For candidates following the Short, Long and Full-training Pathway, the Gateway Review can take place at any appropriate time during your pathway. Your provider will notify you when this will be. For candidates following the Validation Pathway only and who by entry requirement will be experienced Early Years practitioners, preparation for Gateway Review will be addressed immediately. Regardless of the pathway followed and the timing of the Gateway Review, preparation is crucial to a successful assessment outcome and award of EYP Status. Preparing yourself for assessment is the focus of sections two and three of this chapter. An overview of the four components of the Validation Pathway follows:

1. *Standards reflection.* As a candidate you will be required to submit some written work, called a Standards reflection, prior to Gateway Review. This work draws on your analysis of identified strengths and areas of weaknesses within your practice against the Standards.

2. *Gateway Review.* At Gateway Review you will take part in four assessed exercises where you will be required to model the role of an EYP. The Gateway Review is an assessment of three key skills which are fundamental to the role an EYP. These 3 skills are the ability:

   – to make decisions based on sound judgement;

   – to lead and support others;

   – to relate to and communicate with others.

   One of the exercises will take the form of a personal interview with an assessor who will discuss your Standards reflection. The Standards reflection and the Gateway Review are the focus of Chapter 5.

3. *The written tasks.* There are seven tasks in total. Within these tasks you will need to write accounts of your practice as you lead and support other practitioners. In Tasks 1, 2 and 3 you will need to demonstrate evidence that you have led and supported your colleagues in their practice with babies, toddlers and young children respectively. In Task 4 you are required to identify and discuss a critical incident where you have had to 'think on your feet'. Look back to the first reflective task in Chapter 2 on page 11 where

you identified such a situation in your practice. Finally, there are three reflective reports that demonstrate your wider professional role and give you the opportunity to provide evidence for any remaining Standards. When writing the tasks for presentation it is crucial that you begin to identify evidence from your practice to support achievement of the Standards. You will be required to produce a documentary file that contains evidence to support your claim for meeting each of the Standards. The evidence in this file can take the form of observations, settings policies, minutes of meetings and any other appropriate documentation. In addition, you will need to organise a tour of your setting and select three people to act as witnesses to support your practice. Chapter 6 supports both your writing of the tasks and identification of all supporting evidence.

4. *The setting visit.* The setting visit gives you the opportunity to provide an oral account to an assessor of your work in relation to the Standards. The structure of the setting visit by an assessor is clearly defined. In brief, the assessor will interview you twice, interview the three witnesses, scrutinise your file and engage in a tour of your setting. The assessor will also require two periods of time to read the documentary file and map your evidence against the Standards. The setting visit is the theme of Chapter 7.

You should now be able to identify the four components of the Validation Pathway. When considering the components it will be useful to remember that:

1. The Standards reflection must be submitted prior to Gateway Review.

2. The written tasks must be submitted prior to the setting visit.

3. The setting visit will always be the final component of validation and hence will conclude your pathway.

4. Consideration of and preparation for the written tasks may start prior to you undertaking Gateway Review.

The role of the assessor

Before moving on to the next section it is useful to consider briefly the role of the assessor.

Your provider will have recruited and trained assessors for their role on the pathways. Providers are required to attend training and development meetings run by CWDC, so ensuring equity and parity of provision across all providers who offer pathways leading to EYP Status. Assessors will have a practice background in the Early Years sector and typically work as lecturers in universities or colleges or as consultants who offer training and support to Early Years practitioners. In time it is expected that assessors will also be drawn from the growing number of EYPs, and Chapter 8 considers this development in the context of your continuing professional development (CPD). Assessors want to offer the best possible service to candidates throughout the assessment process. Of the four exercises at Gateway Review, assessors report how interesting they find the personal interview. The personal interview allows them to explore the candidate's role and its implementation within a setting. Assessors enjoy the experience of the setting visit, during which they relish the opportunity to observe the candidate in the emerging role of the EYP, as the visit unfolds. Assessors do want you as a candidate to succeed, but they are mindful at all times of their responsibility in ensuring the quality of EYPs entering the workforce.

The next section considers what preparation is useful for Gateway Review.

Preparing for the Standards reflection and Gateway Review

This section will identify key support for your preparation of the Standards reflection and the Gateway Review. The crucial document you must refer to throughout the Validation Pathway is *Guidance to the Standards* (CWDC, 2007a). This not only defines the 39 Standards but offers examples of practice in order to meet the Standards. You can draw on these to tease out your understanding and to use as pointers to identify the Standards in your own practice. Chapter 3, Part 1 looked at the role of an EYP and how this role is influential to the successful delivery of the Early Years Foundation Stage. Look back at the practical task on page 25 in Chapter 3, which encouraged you to begin to identify your practice in leading and supporting others against the Standards. Chapter 3, Part 2 set out selected Standards in a different format and offered a complementary approach to deepening your understanding of them and may help you to identify evidence from your practice.

An important issue throughout this journey and beyond is engaging in reflective practice, and it is important that you begin to analyse your own practice in preparation for Gateway Review. There are several things that can help you to begin this process.

You will have been given an EYP Standards Self-Review Notepad by your provider (which you should be able to download). This is intended to be an evolving document chronicling your progress as you identify your practice against the Standards throughout your daily routine. You would be advised to use this Notepad as you work through the suggested reflective tasks in this book. Analysis of the Notepad will give you an extremely useful overview and help you to identify weaknesses or gaps in your practice as well as highlighting where you can identify your strengths. This analysis will also inform how you should target and work on particular areas that you have identified as weak. Mona Naqvi, a pre-school leader who achieved EYP Status in February 2007, comments that:

> *I found the Notepad a very helpful and effective tool in preparing my Standards reflection. Rather than complete as an online document I decided it would be more helpful to print and blow up the page size to A3, so I had more space to record comments and examples from my daily practice; I added and deleted ideas on a daily basis.*

Reflective conversations with a mentor or a critical friend

A further source of help in your preparation may be a mentor or critical friend, and now is the time to draw on their experience to help in both your analysis of practice and your preparation for assessment. A crucial element of a mentor's support is encouraging you to stand back from your practice in order to analyse and reflect upon it. One of the helpful skills identified by Rodd (2006) as associated with effective mentoring is that of 'reflective conversations'. Entering into reflective conversations with your mentor is key to unlocking and developing analysis and reflection in yourself and therefore crucial for demonstrating achievement of the Standards. The most effective mentors are able to help you to remove yourself from the 'heat of the kitchen' and look down upon your practice or see it through the eyes of another. Mona comments that:

> *I found my mentor's support invaluable in meeting the Standards and fulfilling the requirement of the assessment tasks. For example, I was struggling with the last section of tasks, 'How you evaluate your personal learning'. My mentor guided me by suggesting that I could use quotes I have read from documentation, for example from the EYFS or the* Guidance to the Standards. *She further suggested I could relate the evaluation to the setting's policy documents or indicate that this area of my work was an aspect from my Standards reflection which I had addressed through the task and learned from it.*

Analysis of your practice can also be enhanced by 'engaging in reflective dialogue' (Rodd, 2006, p.172) with a 'critical friend', a peer professional who knows your practice well and who, by honestly appraising your work, can help you identify aspects of it you may wish to develop. You will need to find your own critical friend, and this could be a line manager or a colleague who works at the same level as you do. A critical friend, like your mentor, needs to know about what makes for good, effective Early Years practice, but in this case the critical friend can analyse it from almost the same viewpoint. Mona reflects that:

> *My critical friend was a work colleague who was able to help me find some supporting evidence to meet the different Standards. For example, as I worked in a pre-school, I was struggling to find evidence for Standard 9, 'Provide balanced and flexible daily and weekly routines that meet children's needs and enable them to develop and learn', particularly because the examples given in the guidance all related to day care nursery situations. She suggested that I should use the assessor's tour of the setting to emphasise the importance of free flow and child-initiated routine of the pre-school and back it up with a report from the advisory teachers praising the effectiveness of this practice.*

At Gateway Review you will need to demonstrate three skills that are seen as crucial in being able to lead and support others. You demonstrate these through the four exercises which are discussed in detail in Chapter 5. However, in order to prepare, it may be advisable to consider the group of Standards 'Teamwork and collaboration'. These four Standards encompass what it is to be an effective practitioner who can 'work collaboratively and co-operatively with colleagues and other adults to enhance children's welfare, development and learning' (CWDC, 2007a, p.70). To enable you to engage in analysis of whether this is an area of strength in your practice or a weakness, you should draw on documented support from, for example, a record of your recent appraisal or feedback or assessment from any management or leadership training you have recently undertaken. In addition you might ask your critical friend to takes notes of how you interact with colleagues in situations such as staff meetings, discussions with a parent, or an appraisal that you undertake of a colleague. You should at all times remain aware of confidentiality issues in these examples, and ensure permission is obtained from individuals to allow you to progress and take this forward. Such analysis can be helpful not only to preparation for your assessment at Gateway Review, but to the completion of your Standards reflection and to finding supporting evidence from your practice in preparation for the written tasks.

The next section will consider preparation for the written tasks and the setting visit.

Review of policies and frameworks

The written tasks and the setting visit require candidates to produce supporting evidence clearly demonstrating that they can meet the requirements of all 39 Standards. The achievement of all Standards is underpinned by evidence that your practice is informed by secure knowledge and understanding of principles and policies. Drawing on current legislation and policy changes is considered vital for an EYP in demonstrating how relevant underpinning knowledge and understanding inform both their own practice and that of others, so ensuring equity and consistency at both a local and a national level. It is therefore essential to consider, first and foremost, the evidence that is required to support your achievement of the first group of Standards (1–6), 'Knowledge and understanding'. Within these six Standards are listed the policies and range of statutory and non-statutory frameworks that are considered essential to informing and underpinning your practice as an EYP.

The most obvious document is *The Early Years Foundation Stage* (comprising the Statutory Framework and Practice Guidance) (DCSF, 2008a). Standard 1 is entirely devoted to it, and you must provide evidence that you can demonstrate knowledge and understanding of 'The principles and content of the Early Years Foundation Stage and how to put them into practice' (CWDC, 2007a, p.11). Look back to Chapter 2 on page 16, where Andra offered three case studies of how she led and supported her colleagues in the delivery of the EYFS, and note how she referenced to the EYFS in her accounts.

What follow next are two tasks designed to help you to analyse your current under-standing of policies. The first task concerns national policies that inform your practice. The second task concerns local and setting policies that must inform your practice and addresses Standard 5. The list of policies illustrated in the task is not exhaustive.

PRACTICAL TASK

Table 4.1 looks at national policy documentation that will help to support your achievement of Standards 1–6 and hence underpin your achievement throughout all of the Standards. The list of documentation in column 1 is not exhaustive but offers key documentation that you will be expected to be familiar with.

Create a table, as illustrated in Table 4.1, completing column 1 using the examples given and/or other policy documentation of your choice. In column 2, evaluate your working knowledge of this documentation. Use a three-point scale where:

PRACTICAL TASK *continued*

- *1 indicates very good knowledge;*

- *2 indicates adequate knowledge;*

- *3 indicates little knowledge or none at all.*

In column 3, identify where you have drawn on your knowledge and understanding to inform your practice, most particularly when leading and supporting others. In column 4, identify which Standards this evidence might support. One example has been done for you.

Table 4.1 Policy and framework review

Documentation	How familiar am I with this?	Where have I drawn on this documentation to support my practice, particularly in leadership and support of others?	Which Standards will this help me to achieve?
The Early Years Foundation Stage	1	I have delivered two training sessions for colleagues who work with babies concerning baby weaning	1, 2, 10, 26, 33, 34
Every Child Matters			
Common Core			
Common Assessment Framework			
Key Elements of Effective Practice			
The Children's Plan			
Every Parent Matters			

You should view this table as 'work in progress' and you must extend the list of documentation in column 1 as necessary. Try to identify at least three examples of where each policy has informed your practice. Thorough analysis of the extent of your knowledge of policy documentation will reveal any gaps to be addressed in order to support further your practice and achievement of the Standards.

Now repeat this task, drawing on those policies and procedures that are unique to your setting or local authority such as safeguarding children, bullying, and health and safety. Look at Standard 5 for guidance. These policies prove crucial when dealing with unplanned incidents or 'critical incidents', as they are those that you must have at your fingertips to inform any action you take. Remember that it will be your responsibility, as an EYP, to ensure colleagues have a working knowledge of them. These two tasks will support your analysis of how well you have a working knowledge of all relevant policy documentation. From this analysis you will be able to identify areas for development and start to address them.

What follows now is a short case study written by Margaret Dobbs in which she reflects on how she approached preparation for the Validation Pathway and offers a useful insight you may wish to consider.

Preparing to achieve EYPS: a case study by Margaret Dobbs

CASE STUDY

Margaret achieved EYP status in February 2007. Here she reflects on her preparation, and it is useful to have a first-hand account that you can draw on to help you prepare.

Having reached the point where the idea of being an Early Years Professional is a possibility, there comes the process of preparation. It is almost certain that you will be working in a position within the Early Years sector where your role encompasses considerable responsibility, but this will not necessarily be a managerial role within a setting.

All senior Early Years practitioners will be familiar with the Every Child Matters agenda and must now begin to embrace the new Early Years Foundation Stage and prepare to implement it in September 2008. The holistic approach of the new curriculum, from birth to 5, demands a deeper and more reflective practice, which will improve the quality of outcomes for children in all areas of development. As the EYFS is new, the lead practitioners will need to be very conversant with its structure and implications. An in-depth study of the differences and changes of emphasis might be very rewarding. It should help us recognise and understand the individual characteristics and talents of the child. It might help in ensuring that record keeping, which needs to be the tangible, practical expression of the philosophy, values and principles of the setting, is addressing the four themes and underlying principles of the EYFS, throughout

CASE STUDY *continued*

the child's journey. Practitioners must have a deep understanding of these principles and be able to demonstrate them in practice.

Preparation for EYPS treads some common ground with preparing for Ofsted. For instance, you will know the policies and procedures of the setting, both local and national, and be aware of your own role in monitoring and review. The Standards for EYPS not only demand that you have knowledge and understanding of all legislation pertaining to Early Years but that you are involved in the imple-mentation. It does not matter whether you are a childminder in total control of writing your own policies or a practitioner in a large setting, perhaps one of a chain, where policies may be controlled at some distance. You will still be shaping the way the setting operates within the legal framework, doing daily risk assessments within your own working environment and making sure that other staff are aware of their responsibilities for health and safety and the protection of children.

You will need to examine the relationship you enjoy with the families and carers associated with your working environment and ensure that channels of communication are open, secure and beneficial. So too the structure of the team within which you operate: is it working at a level that fosters cooperation? Do you collaborate to provide better outcomes for all the children in your care? You need to think about how you would show this, how you measure the degree of success that is down to your efforts and contribution. The assessment process for EYPS is about you, not your working environment.

Look around the environment you have helped create in the setting and ask yourself: what does this feel like for a child? Why have I arranged it like this? How have I made it welcoming and stimulating? What is it like for families and carers who are coming for the first time? Suppose they do not speak English: is it still so inviting? Perhaps you are an experienced practitioner with many years behind you, or maybe this career path is new to you: what matters is that you make a difference and your contribution should show.

Being a reflective practitioner is vital to the success of this assessment process. The way you engage with children across all the age ranges is the essence of your work, from the moment those children enter your life, as tiny babies or as boisterous 4-year-olds. All the time you spend with them on their learning journey is precious and a privilege. In meeting children's needs, you fulfil your duty of care and your obligation to the family but most importantly you do it for the benefit of the child so that their well-being, learning and development are enriched by your involvement and relationship with them. This is what you do every day; this is what you must evidence in your journey towards EYPS. It is not enough to be able to produce observations, assessments, plans and so on, although of course these are the essential tools of the trade. An EYP needs to go further and try to evidence the intangible, the influence or effect on others. It is

CASE STUDY *continued*

hard to capture all the magic moments that good practice generates, but help is at hand and other people, parents, other professionals or colleagues, are aware of your influence and will undoubtedly be willing to describe your practice and corroborate your claims of meeting the Standards.

The assessment process calls upon you to take a long, deep look at yourself, as a practitioner and at the other roles you may have: how you influence others, how you make a difference to the lives of children and their families, how you will be the driving force of the EYFS. It is a lot to ask, but then again it is the most important job on the planet.

C H A P T E R S U M M A R Y

This chapter has focused on your preparation. It has given you an overview of each of the components that make up the Validation Pathway and set out preparatory reflective tasks. It has encouraged you to engage in analysis of your practice and has suggested strategies for this. In doing so you will be able to build on your strengths and target your specific areas for development.

Moving on

Chapter 5 deals with preparation for Gateway Review, including the Standards reflection.

FURTHER READING

Rodd, J. (2006) *Leadership in Early Childhood*, 3rd edition. Maidenhead: Open University Press

The chapters on communication skills, decision making, initiating and implementing change will be helpful.

Every Child Matters: and the Common Core of Skills and knowledge: www.everychildmatters.gov.uk

5 Gateway Review

CHAPTER OBJECTIVES

By the end of this chapter you will have:
- explored and analysed key aspects of your role and responsibilities;
- mapped defined skills against your practice and the EYP Standards;
- explored the component requirements of the Gateway Review;
- identified potential areas for development or enhancement in readiness for undertaking a Gateway Review.

The Gateway Review is a 'review of the key skills fundamental to someone aspiring to be awarded EYP Status' (CWDC, 2007c, p.6.). This chapter looks at how to prepare your Standards reflection and defines and considers the three assessed skills which are seen as crucial to your ability to demonstrate the role of an EYP. The chapter explores the four exercises which you, as a candidate, will undertake at the Review and draws on the accounts of previous candidates' preparations and experiences to illustrate the process of undertaking the Gateway Review.

Introduction

The Gateway Review is one of the components of the Validation Pathway. At Gateway Review you will be required to demonstrate evidence of key professional skills necessary for achievement of EYP Status. The four exercises that make up the Gateway Review are the same regardless of the training pathway you follow or your choice of training provider. However, as explained in Chapter 4, the timing of Gateway Review may vary dependent on the pathway you follow.

The Children's Workforce Development Council (CWDC) prescribes the elements of each stage and delivers national training for providers to ensure 'consistency and equality of opportunity, irrespective of where candidates are trained and assessed' (CWDC, 2007c, p.5). Exploration of the requirements for Gateway Review (as listed in the objectives above) and subsequent assessment stages is therefore possible, as the methodology of assessment is identical throughout all assessment centres.

Key characteristics of the role of an EYP are the necessary leadership skills and other professional qualities, which were considered in Chapter 2, to 'make a real difference to your colleagues and the children in your care' (CWDC, 2006b, p.8). The EYP improves practice in their setting by changing practice in their setting. At Gateway Review, as a candidate you will undertake four exercises in which you model the role of an EYP. In doing so you must demonstrate the three skills that are indicative of the ability to lead, support and develop the practice of others. The three generic skills, with exemplification of how they can be demonstrated, are as follows:

1. The ability to make decisions based on sound judgement:

    - thinks beyond the immediate problem and avoids 'quick fix' solutions;

    - concentrates on what is the most important thing;

    - makes appropriate decisions, using the available information but seeking further information when necessary;

    - bases decisions on agreed principles and policies.

2. The ability to lead and support others:

    - gets ideas agreed, whether one's own or those of others;

    - improves practice by motivating others to achieve agreed aims;

    - recognises and develops the potential of others;

    - proposes clear strategies for improvement as a change agent.

3. The ability to relate to, and communicate with, others:

    - communicates clearly both orally and in writing;

    - listens to others' concerns and responds appropriately;

    - shows respect for others in a sensitive manner;

    - manages own feelings and needs.

(Adapted from CWDC, 2007b, p.9)

The Common Core of Knowledge and Skills (DfES, 2005a) defines 'effective communication and engagement' as one of the skills and areas of expertise required by all practitioners within the children's workforce. In many ways this definition neatly encapsulates the three skills listed above. Further consideration of the exemplification of each of the skills in the following sections of this chapter will give you clear and targeted pointers to what assessors at Gateway Review will be looking for. Simplistically, each of the three skills addresses a specific area of expertise that is seen as intrinsic to the role of an EYP. Without these skills, EYPs would not be able to function in the role that is envisaged by CWDC. They would not therefore, become conduits for change.

These three skills are likely to have developed from your extensive day-to-day practice with colleagues in Early Years settings and may have been extended through participation in specific leadership or management training. For those candidates who are following the

Full-training Pathway, they have been identified as transferable skills honed from complementary spheres of practice. It must be evident at Gateway Review through the demonstration of the three key skills that your leadership and support of colleagues are rooted within national and local frameworks and that you model good practice for colleagues at all times. The reflective tasks in Chapter 4 helped you analyse your understanding of national and local policies.

Throughout the rest of this chapter, three EYPs offer accounts of their preparation for Gateway Review. You can read a brief pen portrait of each of them at the end of the chapter.

You now need to begin to identify the deployment of these skills within your current role. In the reflective task below you will reflect on your own practice, focusing on your interactions with colleagues, and consider how you demonstrate the skills as you go about your daily routine.

REFLECTIVE TASK

The three skills and my role

In preparation for identifying these skills within your practice, record a log of daily events (see Table 5.1 below) that captures, for example, when you have:

1. arranged cover for an absent colleague;

2. provided a brief induction for a temporary colleague;

3. responded to a phone call from a worried parent;

4. rung the local authority advisor regarding training;

5. mopped up a puddle from a tap overflow;

6. reminded all colleagues to ensure children are supervised in the toilets.

Look back at the three skills listed on page 49.

Which of the skills did your action(s) draw on? What policy or procedures informed your practice? Were there any implications that you needed to address with colleagues?

Table 5.1 Incident record

Event or incident	Skill 1	Skill 2	Skill 3	Policy/ies	Leadership and support
Tap left on causing overflow	I had to quickly clear water from floor	I identified the necessity to change practice		Health and safety	Immediately circulated memo to all staff regarding H&S

After undertaking the task above Sheri reflects as follows in this extract.

> *It is important you recognise the application of these skills within your role. Consider carefully how you lead and support your colleagues. Reflect on all decisions you make and evaluate the outcome. Ensure that your written communication is clear and grammatically correct. At all times be aware that these three skills are fundamental to your ability in the role of an EYP to lead and support others in the role of an EYP.*

Preparation for Gateway Review

The Gateway Review comprises four exercises and a written reflection. The four exercises in the Gateway Review are based on similar assessment practice in other communities of professionals (such as health and education) that has been found to be both effective and successful. This helps support the 'professionalism' of the Early Years workforce by drawing on effective assessment methodology in other professions.

At Gateway Review, the four exercises involve you modelling the role of an EYP by:

- undertaking a personal interview with an assessor which includes the exploration of your progress in meeting the Standards;

- conducting an interview with a colleague;

- dealing with a series of unforeseen events at the start of a working day; and

- working within a group.

The exercises draw on real-life scenarios typically encountered in the work of an EYP and are designed to offer you multiple opportunities to demonstrate the three skills. Gateway Review does not require you to provide evidence of your practice against each of the 39 Standards. This is required in part 2 of the assessment process and discussed in Chapters 6 and 7. Rather, the Gateway Review seeks to confirm that you as a candidate:

- are developing a good working knowledge and understanding of the Standards;

- have carefully considered and reflected on how the role and responsibilities of an EYP meet the Standards; and

- possess the three skills that are fundamental to the achievement of EYP Status.

After you have undertaken all four exercises and before you leave, you will be asked to write a short written reflection on your experience. This does not contribute to the outcome of your assessment; rather it gives feedback to your provider on how best to support your progress through the pathway. You will be able to draw on your reflection in discussions with your mentor or tutor during preparation for the final assessment stage. For example, Carrie reflected that the experience had made her focus on her leadership skills. She recognised the need to become more proactive in decision making rather than leaving things to see if they resolved themselves.

Before you attend your Gateway Review you will need to:

- prepare and submit your Standards reflection, which is one of the components of the Validation Pathway;

- prepare a short talk for the group exercise. This will be considered later in the chapter.

The Standards reflection

The Standards reflection is a piece of written work where you appraise all aspects of your 'recent' Early Years practice and map these against the groups of Standards. It requires you to think about which groups of Standards you are confident about and which you are less confident about. Think back to Chapter 3, which considered how the 39 Standards are organised into six groups. It discussed how there are clear intentional links between the Standards and suggested of ways of mapping your practice against the Standards. Doing this helped you begin identifying where you feel your practice is strong as well as identifying gaps in your practice. The Standards reflection requires you to consider what else needs to be done in order to fill the 'missing gaps'. The resulting written submission will form the basis of the discussion between you and the assessor during the personal interview.

An analysis of your 'recent' role is another good starting point for preparing your Standards reflection. (Look back at your notes from the tasks in Chapter 2.) By thinking about your key responsibilities and daily practice you should be able to identify good practice and link it to one or more of the groups of Standards. For example, Sheri writes in her reflection:

> *I am confident about my relationships with children (S25–S28). I am excellent at engaging each child, especially during group activities, and always ensure each has a fair opportunity to contribute.*

This information provides a useful starting point for discussion at the personal interview. The assessor could ask Sheri to describe how she undertook her planning and delivery of a group activity and how she ensured that individual children contributed.

Similarly, Maggie writes:

> *I am confident about Standards 29–32, 'Communicating in partnership with families and carers'. I talk to the parents on a 'meet and greet' level and feel this is a far more positive approach than putting carers/parents on the spot with home visits.*

Here the assessor might explore why Maggie contrasts her approach with that of home visits.

REFLECTIVE TASK

Think about what theoretical perspective or research Maggie might have drawn on to inform her practice. How would she evaluate its success?

What it is important to recognise is that neither Sheri nor Maggie detail specific evidence against an individual Standard, as this is not what is required in the Standards reflection. During the interview, assessors will explore with candidates their deeper understanding of the Standards, thereby facilitating candidates' ability to match evidence to individual Standards. In the example above, Sheri's detail of her planning and delivery could later provide evidence for Standard 27, 'Listen to children, pay attention to what they say and value and respect their views.'

The Standards reflection also requires candidates to describe groups of Standards they feel less confident about. Carrie, who has followed the Full-training Pathway (FTP), wrote that she was less confident about Standards 37–39. She writes:

> *Though secure in my development to date, I have difficulties in finding opportunities where I could lead my colleagues in their professional development. All members of my team in the Nursery are ambitious and experienced professionals.*

Identifying a gap in practice such as this is not indicative of failure. Indeed, as reflective practitioners we constantly seek opportunities to re-evaluate and then refine our skills, as well as being open to developing new skills as appropriate. During the interview the assessor could explore how Carrie might draw on aspects of her own professional development, so presenting opportunities for her to interact with colleagues and extend their development. She may need to look to opportunities for this beyond the boundary of the team she belongs to and perhaps even into the wider community of EY practitioners (this was discussed in Chapter 2). Candidates like Carrie who have followed the FTP bring with them transferable skills that were honed in varied and diverse workplaces. Identifying gaps in practice and considering ways in which these can be bridged by reflecting on your own skills and experiences to date are both intrinsic to the roles of a reflective practitioner and an emerging EYP.

The final two sections of the Standards reflection require you to describe how you would build on your strengths and plan what you need to do to address the gaps. A typical example of this might be to extend your practice with babies, which would require targeted work time in the baby room or if necessary in a complementary Early Years setting. Assessors will be looking for candidates 'to do something about' what they have identified as missing in their practice, which in turn must be achievable within the time frame of the assessment process. Sheri identified weaknesses within her practice relating to working in partnership with families and carers (Standards 29–32). She writes: 'I have approached a colleague in my setting who has agreed that I can spend time with her at the beginnings and ends of the day to observe her good practice.'

PRACTICAL TASK

Start a log book in which you record aspects of your daily practice under the following headings.

- *'Working with babies'.*
- *'Working with toddlers'.*

REFLECTIVE TASK *continued*

- *'Working with young children'.*

- *'Leading and supporting colleagues'.*

- *'Working with parents'.*

Consider the 'group headings' for the Standards and transfer or map your practice under these. Identify your current strengths and note any areas of weakness.

Your Standards reflection needs to be an empowering document in which you appraise your practice and identify both your strengths and your weaknesses in relation to the groups of Standards. You will have reflected on how to build on your strengths and address your weaknesses. You will have set a tight but achievable time frame for this. Your Standards reflection must be submitted to your provider before you attend Gateway Review. Note: there is one other preparatory task of preparing a short talk. The requirements for this are explained later in the chapter in the section entitled 'The group exercise'.

Structure of the Gateway Review

The Gateway Review consists of the four assessed exercises and a final written reflection as outlined above. Gateway Reviews are organised by your provider, last for a maximum of half a day and take place in assessment centres. Usually eight candidates are invited to attend a Gateway Review.

You will have already submitted a Standards reflection and prepared a four-minute talk for the group exercise (discussed on page 57). Throughout all four exercises, assessors will be looking for evidence of the three skills that are intrinsic to the role of an EYP in leading and supporting others. You must model the role of an EYP throughout the exercises, but will be most able to demonstrate this in the staff, group and written exercises. General preparation for the Gateway Review should include you familiarising yourself with your Standards reflection, having a good working knowledge of the Standards and having an awareness of the three skills to be assessed.

The personal interview (30 minutes)

Assessors will have received Candidates' Standards Reviews in advance and will be able to explore practice from a knowledgeable position. Throughout the 30 minute Interview Assessors will ask for points of clarification, explore a Candidate's role in more detail and probe understanding of the Standards. These foci should allow a Candidate to demonstrate the 3 skills through their answers.

(adapted from CWDC, 2007c)

In discussing recent and current practice you should be able to demonstrate the ability to lead and support others. An example of this could be by you describing your organisation or leadership of staff development sessions, particularly if a need was identified. By illustrating your role within team meetings, you could demonstrate that the outcomes of discussion are based on the ability to make sound judgements by describing how you encourage colleagues to explore all possible opportunities and value all contributions that are made. Throughout the interview, assessors will be judging that you have the ability to relate to, and communicate with, others. This is demonstrated by a well-written Standards reflection where you have presented work that is appropriately referenced and of graduate standard. Oral responses to assessors' questions should be considered and thoughtful.

Preparation for the personal interview should involve you identifying elements of your practice that could be discussed in greater detail. An achievable time frame for addressing identified weaknesses needs to be thought through and planned.

Staff interview (15 minutes plus 10 minutes' preparation time)

Candidates conduct a 15 minute interview with a colleague whose role is played by an actor. An Assessor observes and records the content of the Interview. Candidates are given 10 minutes preparation time in which to become familiar with the brief and arrange the Interview room to their liking.

(adapted from CWDC, 2007c)

Typically in the staff interview, 'the candidate' must act as a 'conduit to change' by recognising and addressing the needs of a colleague. This involves you playing the role of an EYP and working towards an agreed solution with a colleague (played by the actor). A key feature of the role of an EYP is that they can change and improve practice in others, and it is with this context in mind that you should conduct the staff interview. You have autonomy over how the interview is conducted, and so within the 10 minutes' preparation time it is vital to organise the seating arrangements and if possible provide liquid refreshment. From the outset assessors will be observing body language and recording dialogue. Your aim is to identify the issue that is of concern to your colleague and then offer a strategy to support a change in their practice.

The staff interview allows ample opportunity for you to demonstrate the three skills. The ability to relate to and communicate with others can be identified by you being sensitive towards the concerns of your colleague and by listening attentively and offering encouragement. Many practitioners can adapt and change their practice if they feel supported to do so, and by offering a colleague additional help you can demonstrate how you have the ability to lead and support others. When a colleague's daily practice diverges widely from the principles and policies of a setting, you can draw on these policies as supporting evidence. For example, it may come to your attention that a colleague was incorrect in their advice to parents over what was considered to be a healthy snack for children to bring with them to the setting. You would be able to refer your colleague to the setting's policy on promoting healthy eating. This both illustrates your good practice and further demonstrates that you have the ability to make decisions based on sound judgement. The staff interview lasts only 15 minutes, and you will need to draw on your organisational skills and your ability to keep to tight timekeeping.

Preparation for the staff interview could involve you reflecting on your interactions with colleagues that are of a more 'formal' nature. The reflective task on page 53 in this chapter will help, as will looking back to your notes from the tasks in Chapter 2. If you have not experienced this in your practice then it is vital that you observe this practice in others. Reflecting on supporting strategies you employed yourself, or observed in others, will provide a useful memory bank to draw on during the interview.

The written exercise (30 minutes)

> Candidates undertake a 30 minute written exercise consisting of five or six items. These can include post-it notes, letters from parents, and reports of telephone conversations. Candidates must respond in writing by stating what they would do, when they would do so and by what means.
>
> (adapted from CWDC, 2007c)

The written exercise is designed to allow you to demonstrate the three skills and draw on your ability to be organised and respond within a tight time frame. There are many common and some unexpected events that need to be dealt with at the start of a day, and you need to demonstrate that you can respond quickly, efficiently and effectively. Complaints from parents, staff absence, leaking water pipes and an unexpected Ofsted visit are quite commonplace, and you should be able to draw on your own experience to demonstrate how you would deal with these issues. Chapter 2 asked you to reflect on how you dealt with the 'unexpected' in your setting. Hopefully less common and yet important are issues that arise concerning health and safety and regrettably child protection. You need to demonstrate you have good working knowledge of policies and procedures relating to these areas, recognising that some areas are rooted in national as well as local frameworks. The ability to prioritise is essential in your response, and by concentrating on the most important issues first you will demonstrate the ability to make decisions based on sound judgement. Issues of poor practice by colleagues should be noted, as well as the need to rectify the practice appropriately. Recognising and developing potential in others, for example through targeted professional updating, will demonstrate your ability to lead and support others. Throughout the written response you need to communicate clearly in standard written English.

Candidates often report that the written exercise demands too much within a short space of time. Maggie writes in her reflection of her concern that she has 'not prioritised the issues correctly' and that 'more time to undertake the exercise would have been beneficial' to her. You will have to think and write quickly. On occasions candidates do not finish the paper. Yet this exercise is neither unfair nor unrealistic. There is rarely the luxury of spending time making a considered response to any issue during a busy working day. Unexpected staff absence at 8 am and a broken window both need addressing immediately. Staff absence has implications for the staff/children ratios, and a broken window may cause injury to a child. A colleague dealing with an unhappy parent who wishes to speak with you may wait, whereas glass splinters on the floor and staff absence in the baby room cannot. What you may wish to consider and reflect on here is which of these two issues you would deal with first and by what means? It is to these real-life scenarios that the written exercise seeks your demonstration of the three skills.

Preparation for the written exercise should be by ensuring you have a good working knowledge of policies and procedures and how they are implemented in your Early Years setting. Look back at the tasks in Chapter 4 on pages 43 and 45. Refer to the log of daily incidents you collected (Chapter 2 on page 11). Ensuring you know how to deal with each one effectively would be a good starting point. Discussion with a colleague as to prioritising them in list form will be useful, and you must ensure that where necessary your prioritisation and action are underpinned by policy and procedure.

The group exercise (30 minutes)

Up to 4 Candidates make a short presentation which focuses on a change to practice they have made in their setting. Together Candidates then discuss the presentations and draw conclusions from them. Accurate timekeeping is essential.

(adapted from CWDC, 2007c)

The group exercise allows you to demonstrate the skill that you can communicate with others, most typically from your own presentation and from your response to other candidates' presentations. This is not to disregard the content of your presentation, where you should illuminate how your decision to make a 'change to practice' was based on the skill of making a sound judgement. In addition, the skill of how you supported others in making the change was underpinned by clear communication with them. Tight timekeeping is essential, and each candidate's presentation must be of four minutes in length, leaving just 14 minutes for a group of four candidates to arrive at some conclusions. Two assessors will observe this exercise and will ensure that the time frame for this exercise is adjusted to match the number of candidates involved. It is important to have ownership of the change you are presenting, as this will give you confidence to speak with authority about it. Candidates who have previously undertaken Gateway Review have given presentations on changes to practice that have included healthy snack time, improved observation technique, the dropping off and collection of children, notice boards for parents, home/setting diaries, etc. The list is seemingly endless. No matter how small the change to practice you are discussing, it is important that you convey ownership of the change and how you implemented it with colleagues in your setting. If possible it would be useful to conclude your presentation with a short evaluation of the effectiveness that this change has made to the quality of provision in your setting.

Sheri chose to present a change she had made to the methodology of staff appraisal. She drew on the research that had led her to make this change, discussed what the implications were for colleagues and gave an evaluation of its success. Sheri reported that the change had enabled her to develop the potential of her colleagues more fully, which in turn demonstrated her own ability to lead and support others. Sheri presented her four-minute talk with confidence, helped by ownership of the change and her understanding of how her change was supported by current successful methodology. She demonstrated finely tuned listening skills together with the ability to draw others into the discussion.

Sheri presented her change with minimal reference to her notes, which helped her, as a candidate, to demonstrate the skill of communicating clearly.

By contrast, Maggie chose to present a change she had made to the collection of children by parents at the end of a session. She detailed how this change in practice had first met with opposition from her colleagues, but by listening to their concerns and working with them towards an agreed solution she was able to implement this change effectively. Maggie demonstrated through the content of her presentation each of the three skills being assessed. In addition she took the lead in organising the timing of the group discussion and nomination of a scribe to record the conclusions. Maggie was careful not to appear dominant, but showed a determination to 'get the job done'.

Candidates following the full-time pathway can have difficulty in identifying a change they have implemented. It is useful to draw on ideas from any complementary course of study that identifies good practice. Mentors and/or a critical friend may also help to identify possible opportunities to explore. Many FTP candidates have opened their presentations by introducing how and where they had developed their idea for change. Treasure baskets, singing sessions with babies and improvements to observation technique have been offered as examples of change. What is important is to ensure that your identified change focuses on a 'change to practice' whose outcome is to improve provision for the children. Changing the position of a wall-mounted heater or the colour of the room decor are very weak examples of a 'change to practice' in your setting.

C H A P T E R   S U M M A R Y

By reading this chapter and undertaking the reflective tasks you should be able to identify the three skills that are assessed at Gateway Review in your daily routine and practice. From the reflective task on page 53 you will have identified how your experience and practice helps to lead and develop the role of your colleagues when working with babies, toddlers and young children. In addition you will have identified strengths and weaknesses in your own practice and have taken steps to rectify the weaknesses. You will now be aware of the four exercises making up Gateway Review and know what preparation is needed for them. Ensure that you read information in the EYP *Candidates' Handbook* in addition to this chapter.

Moving on

The next chapters look at part 2 of the assessment process: preparation for the written tasks and the setting visit.

To support Standards reflection

Anning, A. and Edwards, A. (2006) *Promoting Children's Learning from Birth to Five: developing the new early years professional*. Maidenhead: Open University Press

Bruce, T. (2004) *Developing Learning in Early Childhood*. London: Paul Chapman

CWDC (2008) *Guidance to the Standards for the award of Early Years Professional Status*. London: CWDC

This is the updated version of Guidance to the Standards available from September 2008

Appendix to Chapter 5: pen portraits

Sheri is an experienced EY practitioner who is owner-manager of a private day nursery. She draws on 17 years' experience of working in the EY sector and employs a group of 15 staff in her nursery. She is a graduate and successfully followed the Validation Pathway to achieve EYP status.

Maggie has worked in a variety of EY settings for seven years. She is a qualified teacher who after working in a Reception class was particularly interested in children's experiences of transition from nursery or day care settings to full-time schooling. Thus attracted to working with pre-school children she left teaching and found employment in the EY sector, where she has worked with babies, toddlers and young children. She has successfully followed the Validation route to achieving EYP status and is now seeking work in a multi-disciplinary Children's Centre.

Carrie has a degree in Economics and worked at a supervisory level in a building society for ten years. She has two young children of her own and is an active participant of local parenting groups. She was keen to follow her interest in how young children develop. Carrie followed the Full-time Pathway and gained EYP Status. She is now employed in an advisory capacity by the local authority but retains a one-day-per-week placement in a private day nursery for her own continuing professional development.

6 The written tasks and all the supporting evidence

CHAPTER OBJECTIVES

By the end of this chapter you should:
- understand the nature and contexts of the written tasks;
- have begun to recognise what is meant by supporting evidence in terms of your practice and documentation;
- know how to link the written tasks to the supporting evidence;
- know how the tasks and all supporting evidence are linked to the setting visit.

This chapter looks at the preparation for the written tasks and for identifying appropriate supporting evidence to demonstrate your achievement of the Standards. The written tasks are about your role and how you can demonstrate working as an Early Years Professional within your setting or across a number of settings. The chapter outlines the requirements for each task. You are also advised on sources of documentary evidence to support what you have written. It concludes with a case study written by an EYP who reflects on her preparation for the written tasks. Much of this chapter and Chapter 7 has been influenced and written by two experienced assessors for the award of EYP Status. This chapter and Chapter 7 should be considered together.

Introduction

The written tasks are one of the components of the Validation Pathway. You will be required to submit the tasks to your provider in advance of the setting visit. Preparation of the written tasks may begin before you undertake Gateway Review. Your provider will advise and guide you over this timing.

The purpose of the written tasks is to demonstrate the full range of your skills, knowledge, understanding and experience, all of which contribute to the role of an EYP. It is important that you prepare for your tasks thoroughly – you will be guided through this by your provider when you attend preparation days during your pathway, and further detail is also in the *Candidates' Handbook* (CWDC, 2007b). However, it is important that you begin to consider all aspects of your work and reflect on where you are currently meeting the 39 Standards and where potential gaps might be. To start this process, think back to how you appraised your practice against the groups of Standards in your Standards reflection in preparation for Gateway Review. Feedback from Gateway Review may also have provided you with areas for development which you should now consider. You may wish to look back at Chapter 3, Parts 1 and 2, both of which offer an approach to identifying evidence of your practice against the Standards. The tasks on pages 43 and 45 in Chapter 4 helped you analyse your knowledge and understanding of national and local policies which inform your practice. Finally, in your EYP Standards Self-Review Notepad you will have regularly recorded aspects of your practice against individual Standards.

You are required to write tasks that describe scenarios which cover different aspects of your role. Each task will be independent of the others; each task will meet specific criteria and all of them together will provide strong evidence to demonstrate how you meet the Standards in your day-to-day work. The first three tasks cover the three different age groups where an EYP is expected to lead and support the work of others, i.e. working with babies, toddlers and young children. If you are not currently involved with children in any of these age groups you can draw on relevant work within the 'recent past' (up to three years). Relevant work includes examples of projects or activities you have carried out to improve outcomes for children and examples of occasions where you have led or supported other practitioners.

Task 4 requires you to describe an event, referred to within the tasks as a 'critical incident', where you have had to 'think on your feet' and react to a situation or set of circumstances that were unplanned and unexpected and required immediate decisions and actions. Look back to Chapter 2 on page 11, where the role of the reflective practitioner was explored and the related reflective task asked you to reflect on a recent 'critical incident'.

The final written task – Task 5 – comprises three separate reports based on your routine professional role and practice and may involve children, parents, colleagues or other professionals. These tasks are shorter, and their intention is to ensure you address all the Standards within all the written tasks.

Each of the written tasks requires an element of description, analysis and reflection. You will be asked to say what you would do should the same thing happen again and any learning or actions that were implemented as a result.

Guidance is provided on the word count, and you will be expected to link your practice with theory in order to show the source of your knowledge base and how this informs your practice. Provide a reference list and bibliography as you would for any academic assignment or essay.

Preparation for Tasks 1, 2 and 3 (word count for each task is 1,500–2,000 words)

The first three tasks require you to report on activities which demonstrate how you *lead and support other practitioners* in implementing the Early Years Foundation Stage. They need to be three separate accounts, and it is clearly beneficial if you select three contrasting activities which demonstrate evidence for different groups of Standards. Draw on the guidelines in the appropriate section of the *Candidates' Handbook* (CWDC, 2007b) and remember that it is not simply three accounts of activities that *you* have undertaken related to three different groups of children, but activities which also enable you to show *how* you have led and supported other practitioners.

In order to meet the first group of Standards, 'Knowledge and understanding', Standards 1–6, you need to demonstrate secure knowledge and understanding in a range of areas. The written tasks provide an ideal opportunity to link theory with practical examples and for you to explain how your practice is underpinned by a depth and range of knowledge. Again, draw on the tasks in Chapter 4 on pages 43 and 45 to help you. Using terminology correctly is essential and will help you demonstrate your knowledge of concepts such as 'scaffolding', 'guided participation' and 'schema'.

The three tasks need to focus on each of the three age ranges, which recognises that the ages of the children often do overlap within their groupings. For example, Task 1 focuses on the age range 0–20 months, which is described as babies, Task 2 on the age range 16–36 months, described as toddlers, and Task 3 on the age range 30–60 months, which is described as young children 3–5 years (often referred to as pre-school in many settings). If your tasks cover more than one age group you need to decide which one will be your focus for the scenario you describe.

Each task requires you to report on your chosen activity by following a certain format that is set out in bullet points. Your provider will make available to you electronic templates of the tasks with the format laid out. You are then able to word-process your account for each task directly on to the templates. Refer to the relevant section of the *Candidates' Handbook* (CWDC, 2007b) to make sure you are following the correct procedure. Below is the current format for Task 3 showing edited sections from a sample of a candidate's work. These sections offer a snap-shot of how to approach your writing by giving you pointers as to the content of the sections.

Specific preparation for Task 3
Lead and support other practitioners to implement the EYFS for young children (30–60 months).

- *The nature of the activity*
  '. . . This third task relates to children in the pre-school group . . . My personal ethos for the children, staff and the nursery as a whole is that my role is to enable people "to be the best they can be" and my colleague has responded to this and strives for the best in all that she does with the children, therefore from time to time I will either suggest ideas to develop what is in place or she will ask for support for an area where there is room for improvement. From previous evaluation of a long term (yearly) plan . . .'

- *The age range, in months, of the children directly or indirectly involved*
  'Pre-school 30–60 months'. If the activity is about leading and supporting the practice of a colleague with a child or children, e.g. singing songs together, then it is direct. If the activity is about leading and supporting colleagues, e.g. in enhanced ways of observing a child or children, then it is indirect, as the colleague is 'distanced' from the child or children.

- *What you planned to do and why (rationale)*
'. . . I had worked directly alongside this colleague for a number of years and so had a very good understanding of the way she worked. She asked me to support her in the drawing up of this medium-term plan because it was a topic that she had never covered before; her need was mainly to boost her confidence that her ideas were sound and to provide some starting points for possible learning opportunities.

  'I therefore started with a list of factors that I felt it would be important for her to consider in her planning:

  - her expectations of the topic;
  - taking account of any previous concerns re planning;
  - opportunities for involving children in the planning;
  - opportunities for involving the parents;
  - practical considerations – trips (health and safety issues);
  - reflecting the topic through displays;
  - realisation that it was a great topic for covering many aspects of the EYFS.

  'My rationale behind this planning was my own understanding of the EYFS: the role of the practitioner in facilitating learning and current good practice, KEEP (Key Elements of Effective Practice), which is based on EPPE research and refers to "the importance of the practitioner's role in balancing adult led and child initiated activities, the need to engage in sustained shared thinking and the kinds of interactions that will guide but not dominate children's thinking".

  'The EYFS states that "Good planning is key to making children's learning effective, exciting, varied and progressive" (EYFS, 2007, p.12). . .'

- *What happened when you carried out the work (the outcome for yourself, the children, other members of staff)*
'. . . I encouraged her through discussion to:

  - build on her hope for this topic, that she wanted it to be "real" and not just theoretical;
  - use the opportunity for some shared thinking and planning with the children; through circle time discussions talk to the children about recycling and encourage them to collect some items at home for recycling which they could bring into nursery;

  - . . .'

- *Your assessment of the effectiveness of the activity (were there any long-term effects? Who was it effective for?)*
'. . . The children loved talking about the display and showing their parents all the things that they had included in it.

  'I accompanied the children on their trip to the recycling point and could tell how much they enjoyed the experience and overheard them for days talking about their trip to the "cycling point"!

'A parent accompanied us on the trip and she made a point of telling me how much she had enjoyed it, how well behaved the children were and how well the staff had planned the trip. This also reflects our high expectations of the children and a belief that they would find a trip such as this a valuable and enhancing experience . . .'

- *Your personal learning (you need to explain your reflection on what you did)*
  '. . . I reflected on this topic and how it reflects the general way we deliver care and education to the children. I feel that we embrace the statement in the EYFS that "Play underpins all development and learning for young children" (EYFS, 2007, p.7) . . .'

The above example is an illustration as to how you should approach your writing. Remember that you must also identify your practice against the Standards in each task. The templates for each of the written tasks include a column for recording the Standards. Having written these three tasks, it is recommended that you begin to complete your 'task and evidence grid'. To do this, follow the instructions in the *Candidates' Handbook* (CWDC, 2007b) and take advice from your provider. On-going work on this grid throughout all the tasks will be hugely beneficial, as this will give you a feel for which Standards you have provided evidence of and where your gaps are. Whilst any gaps may not be a major factor in selecting your critical incident for Task 4, they certainly should influence your choices for Task 5.

Preparation for Task 4 (word count 750–1,000 words)

For this task you need to identify an unplanned situation in which you have to 'think on your feet' and respond quickly and professionally. In particular you should try to identify a situation in which you had to take decisive action. This task then requires you to describe what happened, analyse your decision-making process and reflect on the effectiveness of your actions and your personal learning from the incident. Again, look back to the notes you made from the reflective task in Chapter 2 on page 11.

You may find it particularly helpful for this task to discuss your choice of incident with other candidates, colleagues, critical friends or professionals such as your mentor. Clearly the more experience you have had, the wider your range of choices, but it does not need to have been a dramatic or emergency situation. Try to identify a situation in which *your* decisive action demonstrated clear leadership, calm and considered decision making and good communication skills, and where your intervention or action had a positive effect. Your evaluation may even conclude that you might have handled the situation slightly differently with the wisdom of hindsight, but it is important that the incident was one which required you to act quickly and decisively.

As with Tasks 1–3 you will need to consider and follow the format specified on the template and in the appropriate section of the *Candidates' Handbook* (CWDC, 2007b). Note that the format for Task 4 is slightly different, as detailed below:

- how the incident or situation arose and what happened (description);
- who else was involved, including the age, in months, of any children involved (people);
- what options you considered and why (rationale);

- your assessment of the effectiveness of your actions (evaluation and analysis);

- your personal learning.

The *Candidates' Handbook* (CWDC, 2007b) will again provide you with some more clarification, as will your provider during preparation days. Remember to update your task and evidence grid after completing Written Task 4.

Preparation for Tasks 5a, 5b and 5c (word count for each task 500–700 words)

Finally, in Task 5, you have the opportunity to provide three further reflective reports (5a, 5b and 5c) on *situations or events* – not planned activities – which further demonstrate your wider professional role and underpinning knowledge of the sector. This is where it is important to review your partly completed Task and Evidence Grid in order to identify the gaps. These accounts are relatively short by comparison to the word count guidance for the other tasks so they are likely to focus on single events or situations which you can use as exemplars of how you have met specific Standards or groups of Standards. You may, for example, want to bring in situations involving families, colleagues, children or other professionals; they may be examples which cover aspects of inclusion, child protection or work with external agencies. For Task 5 it is also important to analyse, not just to describe or narrate. As before, don't forget to comment on your personal learning in each case.

The format of each of these tasks taken from the appropriate section in the *Candidates' Handbook* (CWDC, 2007b) is as follows:

- a brief description of the situation or event;

- analysis of the situation (impact, effectiveness);

- your personal learning.

Again draw on the *Candidates' Handbook* (CWDC, 2007b) and preparation days held by your provider for guidance. Once again, update your task and evidence grid.

What is now important is that the seven tasks, each relating to a different area, demonstrate through your practice that you have covered all 39 Standards. The Task and Evidence Grid offers you confirmation as to whether you have covered them. The creation of your file of supporting documentary evidence will also help you track coverage of the Standards and make a distinction between strong and weak supporting evidence. This is dealt with in the next section. By the end of the written tasks, your assessor should have a clear picture of you, in your role, in your setting(s). Try to ensure that across the tasks you have achieved a balance of demonstrating your own effective practice with your role in leading and supporting others. The written tasks are also often the best place to demonstrate your knowledge and understanding of, for example, legislation and key theoretical perspectives. So do ensure that you have explained the thinking behind your actions, and the theories that underpin your practice. Once you have completed your written tasks, you can then concentrate on gathering together your file of documentary evidence and other supporting evidence in preparation for the setting visit.

Collecting evidence to support achievement of the Standards

When preparing both for the written tasks and for the tour in the setting visit you will need to consider each of the Standards and decide what kinds of evidence will best demonstrate how you meet them. It is essential that whatever you select represents something that you have done yourself. It is also important that you have a working knowledge of the 39 Standards. Look back if necessary to Chapter 3, Part 2, as well as reading the *Guidance to the Standards* and taking note of the exemplars that are offered to support achievement of each Standard. Supporting evidence to underpin your written tasks is through:

- the creation of a file of supporting documentary evidence;

- a tour of your setting;

- interviews with three witnesses.

Although the tour is part of the setting visit, which is the focus of Chapter 7, it is useful to consider in this chapter what potential opportunities it offers for supporting evidence to meet the Standards. Also, your choice of witnesses must be part of your thinking, as the witnesses should offer support to your practice and come into the category of supporting evidence. In addition you may collect up to five witness statements for your file, and these must also be incorporated into your whole approach of collecting supporting evidence. Look ahead briefly to Section 1 in Chapter 7 to familiarise yourself with the composition of the setting visit.

The supporting documentary evidence file

Your supporting evidence must be relevant and recent, which means it must reflect and be based on your practice within the last three years. It must fit into one A4 ring-binder file. Keep this in mind as you go about collecting and sorting your evidence. The size of the file clearly signposts how much evidence you are expected to produce.

Primary-source evidence is the strongest, such as documentation of a training programme you have devised and delivered. This would be a strong primary source of evidence, for example, for Standard 38. Another related piece of evidence which gives further support for meeting this Standard would be examples of written feedback or evaluations from colleagues who attended the training. These two sources of evidence would support achievement of Standard 38. The written feedback or evaluations from colleagues could additionally provide a primary source of evidence for another Standard, such as Standard 34, where you may have evidence to ensure that colleagues understand how best to meet planned objectives.

In the majority of cases you will find evidence overlaps for meeting one or more Standards. You should avoid attributing any piece of evidence against too many Standards, as this may actually reduce the value of the piece of evidence and make it more difficult for the assessor to regard it against a specific Standard. There is also a time factor to consider, as the assessor will need to cross-reference all your claims. It is best not to 'muddy the waters' – keep your references to Standards as transparent as possible.

As mentioned earlier, you can include a maximum of five witness statements or testimonials as documentary evidence. It is important that they are well written, and it is beneficial for you if they are written on headed letter paper. Scraps of paper do not look very professional and may not appear to be credible. Witness statements can be particularly relevant for a candidate who has recently moved settings or who, as an advisor or development worker, is not based at a permanent setting. It would perhaps be an advantage if witness statements are written by people whom you have not asked to act as witnesses on the day, particularly because this then provides for wide-ranging sources of evidence. However, this is not always necessary or possible, especially if you work in a small setting.

Witness statements can tend to focus on your personal qualities, which do not help to provide evidence against the Standards. The best witness statements will testify to your performance against specific Standards. This can be achieved by you clearly explaining that you need the statement to outline your actions rather than your sympathetic nature! By choosing to include witness statements to provide evidence for specific aspects of your work against the Standards, make sure that the statements can corroborate either a scenario or evidence of effective practice. An example of how evidence is corroborated follows:

CASE STUDY

A sensitive issue was dealt with by a candidate who later received a letter of thanks from the parent. The parent also wrote a witness statement for the candidate in which the parent discussed how the candidate had dealt with the sensitive issue. A witness who was a member of staff corroborated this evidence when interviewed by the assessor, i.e. the assessor was able to draw on the witness statement in the evidence file and further explore this directly through a witness interview – thus strengthening the evidence and confirming that a particular Standard had been met.

Avoid putting lengthy documents in the file – only include policies or sections of policies if they are valid in supporting your evidence – and generally confine yourself to documents that you have created, developed or influenced, as you are demonstrating *your* practice, not the practice of anyone else unless you have had a direct impact on their performance. Direct impact may be demonstrated through documentation that is about mentoring a new member of staff, carrying out an appraisal, delivering training to meet an identified need within the setting or, for example, formulating a policy regarding improvements to working in partnership with parents.

The evidence within the file must support achievement of all 39 Standards. However, it may transpire that one piece of evidence supports more than one of the Standards, as discussed above. Each document should be labelled D1, D2, etc., as demonstrated in the *Candidates' Handbook* (CWDC, 2007b), which you should again refer to in order to complete the Task and Evidence Grid. There is no requirement for the evidence to follow the order of the Standards or groups of Standards, and so it will be in the order which you choose. Your assessor needs to be able to use the Task and Evidence Grid in order to easily locate the evidence in your file and vice versa. The assessor may have to go backwards and forwards several times whilst checking the evidence; therefore it is helpful if your referencing is sound.

The *Candidates' Handbook* when discussing supporting evidence states that 'no standard requires more than two sources' (CWDC, 2007b) – what is more important is that the evidence is considered by the assessor to be 'strong' evidence which leaves no doubt in the assessor's mind that you have met the Standard.

The A4 file must be well organised, enabling the assessor to easily navigate their way around it. You should label each document clearly with the document number and the Standards to which it relates.

It would be helpful if you provide an index of the documents which shows the number, Standards and a brief description if appropriate. You will have entered a 'brief description' on your task and evidence grid, and you can simply create an index to match this document.

Remember that you are 'signposting' the assessor to your evidence, and the easier it is to navigate around the folder the more time is available for the assessor to gather evidence.

REFLECTIVE TASK

The written tasks give you the opportunity to provide the widest possible scope to demonstrate your knowledge, understanding and practice. It is important that the documentary evidence you select reflects the activity you have described within the written tasks and offers supporting evidence that you have met the Standards. Draw on your EYP Standards Self-Review Notepad to help you create and review a checklist of supporting evidence. Where you have given an example or examples of your practice against a Standard, make a note of what evidence you have to support it. Use shorthand notation when helpful, for example D is documentary evidence, W is a witness and WS is a witness statement, T is the tour, etc.

Tour of the setting

Careful planning and preparation for the tour are essential, in order to make the best possible use of the 45 minutes allowed for it. Think about which Standards will be most effectively evidenced by the tour. Make sure you list these on your 'Notes on the Tour of the Setting' form which your provider will supply. You could use bullet points to give a brief description of what will be seen, e.g. planning, displays, parents' notice board. The best tour plans list the Standards in the order they are met on the tour. Think ahead, do a dummy run of your planned tour, and adapt the listing of the Standards appropriately.

Identifying appropriate witnesses

The witness interviews offer an excellent opportunity to present evidence of your practice that cannot so easily be written about or observed on the tour. Try to select credible witnesses who can offer a range of evidence. It is very important that they know you well enough to be able to describe specific examples of how you work – and that they have a high opinion of you and the work that you do! You need to have confidence in your witnesses, and they need to feel confident and comfortable in what they have to say. The best witnesses are often keen to sing your praises, but it is important that they give relevant information which can be used as evidence, so do take time to explain to them what the Early Years Professional Status is all about. It is even more helpful if they have some understanding of the particular Standards that you are hoping will be covered in the interviews.

You should select your witnesses so that they can:

- verify things that you have asserted or claimed in your written tasks or document file;

- provide specific examples of skills you have demonstrated as a colleague, in relation to a child in your care or in relation to multi-disciplinary working.

It is important that at least one of the witnesses has worked with you or been supported by you in the workplace. This type of witness is particularly helpful in providing evidence for the group of Standards 'Teamwork and collaboration' (Standards 33–36). In addition they may be able to verify evidence for the group of Standards 'Relationships with children' (Standards 25–28). If you choose to have two colleagues as witnesses, it may be helpful to have your line manager, who can verify your involvement and level of responsibility within the setting, and a more junior member of staff whom you have led and supported in development of their practice.

It is often helpful to have a witness who is a parent of one of the children attending your setting. This witness may be able to help you achieve Standards within the group 'Communicating and working in partnership with families and carers' (Standards 29–32).

Another potential witness could be drawn from your inter-professional practice, such as a colleague from a complementary discipline such as Health and Social Care. Try to ensure that they can offer additional supporting evidence to that of your other witnesses.

After the witness interviews, you may find it helpful to ask your witnesses if there was anything in particular the assessor asked them – it might give you some clues about which areas the assessor was exploring in their evidence gathering, which may help you prepare for your final interview.

PRACTICAL TASK

Selecting credible witnesses

Begin to think about whom you will choose to be a witness. Start to make a list of potential witnesses from within and outside your setting. This could also inform your choice of witness statements. It may be helpful to do this in a grid, as shown in Table 6.1. Against each person you have listed ask yourself the following questions:

- *How long has the person known me?*

- *Can I rely on their evidence being supportive? If this evidence comes from your line manager or those who work for you, it should be strong and supportive. Have you recently moved jobs and need to draw on a colleague from a previous setting? If they cannot attend on the day as a witness, could they provide a witness statement for you? You can ask for witnesses to be interviewed by telephone. This requires careful planning within the timetable, and think of where the assessor will make the phone call from. Privacy is of paramount importance in such a situation.*

Table 6.1 Identifying and selecting appropriate witnesses

Name of witness	Role	How long have they known me?	How well do they know what I do?	Which Standards do I need them to support?	Are they available on the day?
AA	Nursery manager	Five years	Has been my line manager for three years	S1–6 and to support my role as discussed in Task 1; also S35	Yes
BB	Parent	Two years	I have been the key worker for their daughter	S29–32 and possibly S39	Will have to confirm but will undertake telephone interview
CC	Colleague	One year	CC has worked with me since joining the setting	My effective practice, and relationships with children, but particularly S33, S34 and S36	Yes

Final thoughts

The following scenarios have been offered by candidates reflecting back on how they prepared and considered evidence to support the Standards. They offer useful insight into how you can build on your evidence so it offers more than one opportunity to support your practice:

- 'Standard 10 is about observations linked to planning. You need to ensure that the assessor is aware that evidence will be visible on the tour, where for example planning is displayed on notice boards. You could show the assessor examples of children's personal progress records as you walk around each room or select an example for your document folder.'

- 'Standard 16 is about sustained shared thinking – this may be visible when watching other staff whilst on the tour, engaged with the children and sharing learning through positive interaction. In addition you will need to show your understanding of this and how you promote this within your setting or the settings with which you work. A witness statement may provide useful evidence of how you engage with children and model this practice for others.'

- 'Standard 33 is about establishing a culture of collaborative working. There may be an opportunity for a witness to talk about your work with the adults, but remember that the Standard uses words such as 'establish' and 'sustained', which suggests that the practice must be 'embedded' – you need to be able to prove this.'

What follows is an informative written account by an EYP offering advice on preparation for the written tasks.

Preparing for the written tasks

Below is a case study written by Margaret Dobbs. Margaret achieved EYP status in February 2007, and here she has written an account of how she prepared for the written tasks. In it she clearly demonstrates her thinking and planning during her preparation. She leads you through the groups of Standards and offers excellent advice on the importance of reflecting on your work. She discusses finding evidence for her documentary file.

CASE STUDY

When working through the Guidance to the Standards, *I was being constantly reminded of aspects of my own day-to-day practice. When considering my own examples, I found it a straightforward task to link my practice with several Standards, some met in part, others more fully.*

But where to start and how was I to write written tasks that would cover every Standard in depth for each age group? The word limit is helpful; it guides you to write selectively and concisely and not waste words. I found it more productive to write my thoughts down about various areas of my work and then to think about what Standards may have been met rather than try to write a piece with Standards in the back of my mind. Where you feel you have met a Standard, you need to consider if it has met all the 'must, should and wills' or whether you have to continue trying to fulfil that Standard throughout your work. Some Standards keep coming back again and again and others are hard to pin down in words.

To meet the 'Effective practice' Standards, the activity should be current, within three years, and ideally within the current setting so evidence is easier to come by. When writing about practice, it is easy to fall into the trap of making assumptions: for statements to be assertive rather than exemplary. Examples make for strong evidence. I used an example in

Task 3, where I had led and supported another member of staff who was anxious about carrying out a challenging lesson plan of introducing 3- and 4-year-olds to the concept of the big bang theory. It turned out to be a series of wonderful sessions with exploding black balloons full of glitter, children dancing to exciting music and coloured streamers as cosmic dust and, as we worked our way through it, my colleague saw how, despite her best-laid plans, the children led us into the best way to represent her ideas as they became 'planets' and 'erupting volcanoes' with such energy and enthusiasm that her evaluation of the activity was over three pages long. My skill as an EYP was to reassure but not intimidate, facilitate and encourage, and help her understand that flexibility and allowing oneself to follow the lead of the child will always be the most rewarding in terms of the children's learning and our own. This activity proved so popular that many of the parents became involved because their children had been reliving their experiences at home. I found myself being able to evidence more Standards because of the way the activity evolved. Individual children took their learning into different directions and it became a massive topic on the solar system and evolution, with learning outcomes far beyond what was originally planned. My input at the early planning stage was helping my colleague to differentiate the activity to include all the children, one of whom had profound physical difficulties and another who was frightened of balloons.

It is particularly tricky to evidence relationships with children. It seems strange when this is almost certainly the most important part of being an EYP. The tasks will demand some detail of planning and resourcing, but these are easily evidenced, after all, through paperwork and in context. How do we show, for instance, that when we communicate with children we do so calmly and with respect, responding appropriately and fairly, asking questions at the right level, perhaps using touch or signing, empowering the child to feel confident to respond, affirming their identity, listening to them and acting on what they tell us? This is what needs to be written down, the details of what was said and how it was done, to show that children were listened to and taken seriously or were perhaps engaged in sustained shared thinking. Also, how do we encourage other practitioners to share the same commitment to communicate with children in this way? Role modelling is just the start; the measure of the effectiveness is seeing consistent good practice in others and the creation of an emotionally literate environment where children feel confident in communicating and find channels in which to do so. It does not stop there, of course, because, alongside the development of good relationships with children, Standards are being met through the teamwork that supports those relationships, the effective practice which develops those relationships and the working partnership with parents which will enrich those relationships.

It is really important, then, that the written tasks reflect not only the three age groups but your own practice, your leadership and support of others and sound links to the curriculum. They should demonstrate knowledge and understanding, using references to appropriate research or study and the philosophy, values and beliefs that underpin practice. With the tasks there is a section for personal learning. It is through this reflection that the level 6 quality of the written work can often be seen.

By ensuring that the content of the seven written tasks claims every Standard in range and depth, the setting visit that follows is made easier for the assessor and far more likely to be successful. Standards that you have claimed must be evidenced on the visit. This can be done by documents such as planning sheets, observations, assessments, children's records, diary entries and children's work. There may also be staff meeting minutes, advisors' notes, letters from other professionals, letters from parents, witness statements from practitioners and photographs, subject to the usual permissions. The documentary file never leaves the premises but should be anonymised. The paper evidence is not the be-all and end-all and, by its nature, paperwork can only say so much. Witness interviews are verbal testimonies which again verify your claims and can be most useful, for instance a member of your team might discuss how you helped her map out her CPD for the coming year. The assessor will be able to probe for the extra examples of practice that will help clinch the Standard. The personal touch is when the assessor is taken around the setting on the tour. During those precious 45 minutes, the impact of you, the EYP candidate, should be very much in evidence, those essential qualities of being the driving force behind the EYFS and the agent of change who has identified what needed to be improved or enriched and has already done something about it.

C H A P T E R   S U M M A R Y

This chapter has discussed how you must think about your practice in order to choose the best possible activities for your written tasks. You must remember that within all the tasks a common theme is writing about how you lead and support others to develop their practice. It further advised on what is strong evidence to support your written work and to achieve the Standards. It looked at how some Standards need to be broken down into parts and how each part requires its own supporting evidence. When beginning to compile your documentary file you must refer to the *Candidates' Handbook* (CWDC, 2007b) at all times and any additional advice or information provided by your provider. In collecting your evidence it also considered the role of the witnesses and how best to select them.

Moving on

The writing of the tasks and the collection of all supporting evidence is inextricably linked to the setting visit. Now read Chapter 7 about the setting visit.

FURTHER READING

Redman, P. *et al.* (2001) *Good Essay Writing*, 2nd edition. Maidenhead: The Open University.

DCSF (2008) Leading and managing Children's Services in England: a national professional development framework: http://www.dfes.gov.uk/publications/childrensplan/downloads/7483-DCFS-Lead%20&%20Manage.pdf

7 The setting visit

CHAPTER OBJECTIVES

By the end of this chapter you should be able to:
- identify and understand the elements of the setting visit;
- clarify the requirements for each element;
- begin to consider the evidence you will need to collect;
- identify the people you may wish to involve in the setting visit.

The setting visit is the final stage of the assessment process. For you, the candidate, it is the opportunity to demonstrate your achievement of the EYP Standards through both oral and documentary evidence. Your training provider will have selected an assessor, who will visit you in your setting. The assessor's role is to seek verification that you have met the Standards through scrutiny of your document file and interviews with both you and your selected witnesses. The chapter in its entirety is to help you plan for the requirements of the setting visit. It sets out the elements of the setting visit, essential preparation and how best you can prepare for a successful outcome.

The elements of the setting visit

You will now have completed and submitted the written tasks, as discussed in Chapter 6. In addition you will have submitted to your provider all other supporting documentation, which to date includes the following.

1. Your Task and Evidence Grid (which was considered in Chapter 6);

2. Your Notes on the Tour of the Setting (which was considered in Chapter 6);

3. Your Setting Visit Form, which includes a timetable for the visit.

You should check in the current *Candidates' Handbook* (CWDC, 2007b) regarding all relevant documentation you must complete and submit to your provider prior to the setting visit. All references to the *Candidates' Handbook* are current as at the time of writing. Readers should always check with their provider and the latest documents from CWDC.

The Setting Visit Form gives full administrative and contact information about you and your setting. It must also include the names of your three witnesses and their relationship to you, such as colleague or parent of a child in your setting. The selection of suitable witnesses is discussed in Chapter 6. This is also addressed in the *Candidates' Handbook* (CWDC, 2007b), and you should ensure that you have read this section.

Your provider will have briefed you on the required documentation and set a time frame for its completion and submission to them. In addition they will have appointed your assessor, who will read and assess your written tasks before the setting visit. The assessor will set the date for the visit 'where possible giving a minimum of seven working days notice' (CWDC, 2007b, p.17).

Assessors will spend up to six hours in your setting. During this time they are required to follow a prescribed timetable and will report back to your provider on whether or not this has happened. It is up to you, the candidate, to organise this timetable. Table 7.1 shows an example based on that in the current *Candidates' Handbook* (CWDC, 2007b). Your timetable for the setting visit must be organised in a similar pattern, and this must be sent to your provider before the setting visit. The start time is agreed following negotiation with your assessor, but the duration of the setting visit and the order of the elements will normally be unchanged. Deviation from the prescribed timetable can only be with the permission of your provider and/or visiting assessor. If an unforeseen occurrence happens immediately prior to the visit or during it, assessors will make allowances for this and will adapt. Your role in managing such an event will contribute to how the assessor views you in the role as an Early Years Professional, as one who can respond quickly and efficiently to such an occurrence.

The individual elements of a setting visit timetable are now briefly examined.

The initial interview with you relating to the Standards

In the initial interview the assessor will draw on your written tasks as the basis for discussion. The assessor may ask for clarification or ask you to expand on what you have written.

Table 7.1 Example of a Setting Visit timetable

8.20	Arrival of the assessor: meet the candidate and the setting manager if appropriate
8.30	Your first interview with the assessor
8.50	You explain the organisation of your file of supporting evidence
9.00	Scrutiny of your file by the assessor
10.15	Tour of the setting
11.00	Assessor's writing and reflection time
11.30	Witness interviews
12.30	Lunch
13.00	Assessor's writing and reflection time
13.30	Your second interview with the assessor
14.00	Visit concluded

Adapted from CWDC (2007b), p.18

CASE STUDY

A candidate in Task 3 had described an activity which included encouraging a group of 4-year-olds to express their feelings and opinions about their setting. In order to link this effectively to Standard 27, the assessor asked how the candidate might lead and support colleagues to value and respect the views of younger children and children with communication difficulties, thereby drawing on a wider range of supporting evidence for this Standard.

Scrutiny of your file of documentary evidence

Following on from this, the assessor will then scrutinise your file of documentary evidence. This was discussed in Chapter 6. The assessor will be looking for additional evidence to support your achievement of the Standards. For example, during the interview the assessor may have asked you about an action which was agreed within your team. If the decision and agreement were made at a staff meeting, minutes or notes from the meeting would be useful evidence for the assessor to scrutinise in your file to support your account.

A tour of your setting

The assessor will then undertake the tour of the setting (see Chapter 6). They will not want to discuss aspects of your role with colleagues during this tour. Rather the assessor will want to see further evidence to support your achievement of the Standards. To support Standard 9, for example, you may wish to show the assessor evidence of weekly schedules, routines or plans on relevant notice boards. Supporting evidence for Standard 10, for example, might be from copies of observations by colleagues, but work in progress is even better. On some occasions assessors are able to see staff making notes (on sticky notes or in notebooks) during the tour – but, as always, you need to be able to demonstrate your influence on this practice. You should also consider how you interact with colleagues, children and others as you conduct the tour. Opportunities for interaction with children may present themselves whilst on the tour, which will contribute to your evidence for Standard 27, although this needs to be natural, not artificial. Similarly, a parent wanting your attention at some point on your tour may be an inconvenience, but if handled sensitively and effectively may provide additional evidence for Standard 30.

Interviews with witnesses who are familiar with your work

The assessor will then conduct three interviews with witnesses. You choose who these witnesses are and you brief them as to the reasons for their selection. As previously discussed in Chapter 6, you need the three witnesses to provide the widest possible evidence base to support demonstration of your achievement against the Standards. Further explicit information on who is eligible to act as your witness is explained in the *Candidates' Handbook* (CWDC, 2007b), which you should refer to.

The assessor's writing and reflection time

From the timetable you will notice that two periods of private reflection are allocated for the assessor: one before the witness interviews and one before the second, that is the final, interview with you, the candidate. In the first the assessor is able to take time to write up notes and reflect on what they have seen and heard in the tour. They will also prepare for the interviews with the witnesses. During the second period of writing and reflection time the assessor will prepare the focus of the final interview with you.

The final interview with you relating to the Standards

During this final interview the assessor will ask for any points of clarification and use it to 'mop up' missing or incomplete evidence of your achievement of the Standards. An illustration of this for Standard 7 is that the assessor may ask how you would encourage other practitioners to extend children's learning, for example with a child who was particularly able. This would suggest that the assessor has already documented where you have evidenced your own high expectations of children, but they are seeking additional or corroborating verification of how you lead and support others in their practice. It may be useful to think back to Chapter 3, Part 2, which looked at how Standards can be made up of several parts and how to ensure that you demonstrate evidence for each part.

This section has briefly discussed each element within a setting visit and how you must organise a timetable for the setting visit. The next section looks in more detail at how to prepare for the setting visit.

Preparing for the setting visit

Thorough preparation is key to a successful outcome. This section and Section 3 are intended to help you prepare for the day by reflecting on all the elements that constitute the setting visit. It has been written by two experienced assessors for the award of Early Years Professional Status. They offer their perspective of what assessors are 'looking for' from candidates throughout the setting visit. They also offer 'key considerations' which will be helpful to your preparation and planning of the visit.

Setting the scene

The main purpose of the setting visit is to complete the picture. Your Gateway Review will have demonstrated a snap-shot of your skills, abilities and experience. Now is the time to show yourself as a 'complete' Early Years Professional!

Your provider will have forwarded your tasks to the appointed assessor at least one week prior to the date of the setting visit. The assessor will scrutinise these in detail in preparation for the visit and will draw on their content for the first personal interview. It is important that the tasks are written carefully and concisely, leaving your assessor in no doubt about what evidence you are demonstrating. The evidence within the tasks will link to documents in your document folder, and these links will also be the focus for some discussion. You will have also documented that some evidence will be visible when you take your assessor on the tour of the setting, as well as when the assessor interviews your chosen witnesses. A final interview with you will be when the assessor attempts to tie up any loose ends regarding evidence to support achievement of the 39 Standards. It is from this combined evidence that the assessor will gain insight into the 'bigger picture' of you in the role of an Early Years Professional.

Identifying and selecting evidence to support you in achieving the 39 Standards has been highlighted and discussed throughout all the preceding chapters but most particularly in Chapters 2, 3 and 6. Chapter 6 discussed the nature of good supporting evidence for achievement of the Standards and how to reference this and link it into your written tasks and to the tour and in identifying who will best act as your witnesses.

PRACTICAL TASK

Self-assessment task

Take time now to review your EYP Standards Self-Review Notepad. In your Notepad you should have been identifying your practice against the Standards and identifying evidence to support your achievement of them. Think back to Chapter 6, where the nature and type of evidence were discussed. Ask yourself the following questions:

- *How will I address gaps in my practice or supporting evidence?*

- *Is my documentary evidence current?*

- *Is my evidence strong?*

- *Is my evidence reliable?*

In Section 3 of this chapter when discussing the tour, an example is given where the supporting evidence was unreliable. Look ahead to page 82 and read this now. The candidate had not prepared sufficiently well and was let down by their colleague and the nature of the supporting evidence.

Considering accommodation suitable for the assessor

You are expected to find a room for the assessor to use for the entire time that they are in your setting. This may be difficult to organise in some settings but it is a requirement and cannot be compromised. Possible solutions are that you may be able to use a room close to the setting, whether adjacent, attached or within a building on the same site.

The setting visit may well mean some disruption for your colleagues. An example may be if you have to take over the staff room for the day. However, the situation needs to be managed as best as you are able. The assessor will be aware of the way you organise the day. Effective organisation will reflect on your conduct as a professional and help to form a good impression of you as an Early Years Professional.

In our experience, rooms used have ranged from dedicated meeting and/or interview rooms in Children's Centres to offices within a county council building. Staff rooms have been used, and occasionally classrooms have been made available for the day.

Key consideration: Once you have found a room you then need to ensure that this is made as comfortable as possible in terms of seating. There will need to be at least two chairs – one for the assessor and one for yourself and witnesses to use during the interviews.

A table should be available, as the assessor will have a great deal of paperwork to complete throughout the day. There have been occasions when assessors have had to sit on low chairs and complete the documentation on their knees. This is far from ideal and should be avoided.

You must also endeavour to ensure that there will not be any interruptions or 'through traffic', as this would be extremely distracting – both for the assessor and for anyone who was being interviewed at the time.

You are not expected to provide meals, but a constant supply of water and the offer of tea or coffee will be appreciated by the assessor. In some circumstances candidates have told assessors that they may use the kitchen to make their own drinks, but this is not best practice. The day follows a very tight time schedule and the assessor does not have the time to do this. It could also be difficult from a social perspective, as people are often chatting whilst making coffee, and the assessor needs to remain distanced from interaction with your colleagues.

Some settings do offer lunch to assessors, but this has normally been in settings where lunch for all adults is part of the routine. In these circumstances the meal has been plated and taken to the assessor in the designated room. Assessors usually take the allocated half-hour for the lunch break and in most cases will have brought their own food. Some assessors like to take the opportunity to leave the setting for a short break but generally they remain in the room. Meeting the individual needs of an assessor is something you can have a conversation with them about on arrival.

Assessors will require all of the time allocated within the day and may need a few minutes at the end to gather their belongings. It is important that you are available throughout the visit even if the times vary from your normal hours.

REFLECTIVE TASK

The following task takes the form of a checklist. This is intended to support you in finalising the details for your setting visit. As you read through each question, are you confident that you can answer yes? If you cannot answer yes, make a note that you will address what needs to be done:

- *Have I spoken to relevant colleagues about the requirements of the setting visit?*

- *Have I received assurance that a room can be available during the time the assessor makes the visit?*

REFLECTIVE TASK *continued*

- *Have I thought about the tour of the setting? Have I decided on a good starting point?*

- *Have I completed my notes on the Tour of Setting form? Have I identified evidence and Standards on it?*

- *Have I identified three witnesses who can testify to my practice? Have they indicated a willingness to do this and whether they are likely to be available?*

- *Might I need to set up or negotiate a telephone interview if one of the witnesses is unable to attend?*

- *Have I organised my supporting documentary evidence file? Is each piece of evidence in my file clearly referenced to the Task and Evidence Grid I am sending in?*

This section has considered what you need to consider ahead of the setting visit and what plans you should be making. The next section takes you through the visit step by step, giving clear pointers to what an assessor is looking for.

The setting visit – as it unfolds

Arrival

When your assessor arrives you have ten minutes to make initial introductions.

Key consideration: You need to decide in advance who you think are the relevant colleagues to introduce at that time – usually the setting manager or colleague in charge (if it is not yourself). Occasionally candidates have introduced the witnesses, but this is not necessary.

The first interview with the candidate (20 minutes in length)

The following points are intended to help you reflect on your approach to this first interview:

- Give clear and concise answers; the assessor has to write down your responses (as near verbatim as possible), so avoid rushing them – take your time and think about what you are saying. Try to keep to the point.

- The interview allows you to fully explain your role and responsibilities within the setting and focuses on gaining evidence and clarity around you as an Early Years Professional being responsible for supporting and leading colleagues in the implementation of the Early Years Foundation Stage (DCSF, 2008a) within your setting. The assessor will want to know if as part of your role you:

  - impact on and influence children's care, learning and development;

- lead and support the training or mentoring of new or existing staff;

- lead and support review of practice or collaborate with colleagues regarding, for example, observation, planning and assessment;

- cascade changes or make updates to policy or procedures;

- carry out appraisals.

- The assessor will ask you questions relating to your written tasks and will be seeking from you clarification and expansion on what you have written – this is your first opportunity to explain anything that the assessor feels is unclear within the written tasks. In addition, there may be events which you find easier to talk about in person or to expand on activities you have described within the tasks. It may be helpful, for example, to explain how a decision you made in relation to your critical incident was influenced by your knowledge of a child's family background or history.

- The assessor will be looking for further supporting evidence throughout the interview on how you are meeting the Standards that you have claimed within the tasks. You might, for example, be able to explain how your knowledge and understanding of legal requirements or national or setting policies influenced your rationale in one of your tasks, thereby helping to demonstrate evidence for Standard 5. Make sure you take the full opportunity to expand on your role relating to your practice and leadership and support of colleagues.

Scrutiny of the document file

You have ten minutes to describe to the assessor how you have organised your document file. The assessor will scrutinise the file for 75 minutes. Preparation of this file was discussed in Chapter 6.

Key consideration: Remember, once you have left the room the assessor only has your file to refer to!

Tour (45 minutes in length)

Do remember that it is not the setting that is being assessed – it is you! This means that a setting that clearly presents as high-quality provision will not necessarily be sufficient in itself to prove your abilities – you need to demonstrate your influence and impact within it. Similarly, a setting which has weaknesses which you are working to improve may still provide sufficient evidence, if you can demonstrate your positive influence within it. If you are responsible for more than one setting, for example, it is sometimes easier to demonstrate your influence on practice within one that has seen significant improvement under your leadership and support rather than one which has always been strong.

When you plan your tour, think about what you will take time to explain as you show the assessor around. In particular, plan to point out things that you have influenced or been responsible for and offer explanations. For example:

- 'I influenced the way this room is organised to allow easier access to the outdoor area.'

- 'I introduced this daily whiteboard as a way of improving the feedback to parents about the range of activities offered during the day, which are not always included on the plans, as they are often child-initiated.'

Key consideration: Try to avoid saying 'We did . . .', as that does not make it clear what you personally have done. It may be good teamwork to share the credit with your colleagues but this is not the time to be modest!

As you conduct the tour, point out plans, records of observations, displays, notice boards and children's work. Your assessor will have looked through your document file, so be prepared to show anything which may have been referred to in that. However, do make sure that you are confident in what you have claimed as your practice and supporting evidence.

CASE STUDY

One candidate had explained in great detail how she had introduced a new way of recording observations in individual books for each child, but she was then unable to find one to show the assessor when asked! Not only did she have to ask another member of staff where the books were kept, but when she found them she discovered that they hadn't been used after the first entry several weeks earlier. This was a missed opportunity to verify what had looked like good evidence for Standard 10.

By contrast an unforeseen but opportune moment during another tour allowed the assessor to observe supporting evidence for this candidate.

CASE STUDY

One unplanned interruption from a child during a tour provided good supporting evidence. The child confidently presented the candidate with a model made from a construction toy and asked her to put it 'on the special shelf' so that she could show her mum when she came to collect her. Not only did the interaction and obvious rapport between the candidate and the child help to verify Standards 25 and 26, but the confidence that the child had in the candidate ensuring that her creation would be valued and kept safe also contributed to Standard 27.

Don't forget the importance of outside play areas during your tour. The assessor will be interested in how and when the children access outdoor facilities, so do ensure you explain this if it is not easily observed on the tour.

Key consideration: If you do not have a dedicated outdoor space you must still find ways of evidencing how your children access outdoor play in accordance with the requirements of the Early Years Foundation Stage (Enabling environments).

Your assessor may not have been involved in your Gateway Review, so you can draw on the example of a change you implemented in your setting which you used for the group exercise. Do not be afraid of repeating it by pointing out and explaining what you did and how. Do concentrate, though, on the areas which are less easily evidenced in the written tasks and interviews.

If on your tour you observe practice or are aware of an incident which you are not happy with, it is unlikely to be an opportune time to deal with it (unless you determine that this is a critical incident that needs your involvement). However, you may want to explain to the assessor what you observed and how you intend to deal with it afterwards. It is important to demonstrate your awareness and understanding of what good practice looks like and how you are developing it in your setting. You need to be able to explain work in progress.

Interview with witnesses (60 minutes in length)

The selection of witnesses has been discussed in Chapter 6. The three witnesses need to be interviewed within a 60-minute time frame. This does not have to be broken down into three 20-minute interviews; rather the length of the interviews should match the amount of information you hope the witnesses will give to the assessor. It is up to you:

- to ensure your witnesses are available at the time agreed (i.e. that cover is arranged if necessary);
- to agree with your witnesses the order in which they will meet with the assessor and the length of time each will be interviewed for.

The final interview with the candidate (30 minutes in length)

Key considerations: Is there anything you want to add? What might the assessor be looking for? Can you prepare for this?

This final mop-up interview allows the assessor to explore further and gain evidence for any Standards that may not have been fully met. They may wish to get clarity on aspects that have cropped up throughout the day – from the witnesses, from the tour or from within the document folder. The assessor could potentially be looking for the following:

- The rationale of why certain evidence was chosen or of practice observed. These questions will relate specifically to what has been seen or discussed throughout the day.
- Greater depth in your knowledge and understanding (Standards 1–6) – this could be pertaining to general childcare-related issues or more specifically around legislation, policy and procedure. The assessor may wish to explore how you keep up to date with an ever-changing sector (Standards 37–39)!
- Additional information about your role in developing partnerships with others, e.g. your influence on aspects of inter-professional practice to support children's transitions (Standard 35) or your relationships with parents and carers in supporting a child who has particular specialist needs (Standards 23, 31).
- The opportunity to fill in any gaps in the evidence you have provided – there may be some quite small issues or areas that the assessor is seeking to resolve that require some form of explicit illustration from the candidate – a tying up of loose ends.

Your assessor will want to be certain that you have fully met all the Standards and will be working hard to verify all of your claims.

Key consideration: Although you cannot specifically prepare for this interview you could make time to review the progress of the day from your own perspective whilst the witness interviews are being held and run through a checklist of all that you had hoped to put across during the visit. If you feel that you have left anything out, this final interview may give you an opportunity to present this to your assessor.

Final words of advice

It is important to remind yourself throughout the day that the role of the Early Years Professional is one that requires a professional approach, and how you organise your day will be a reflection of this. Your preparation is not merely about the physical arrangements but how you have briefed your colleagues. Your conduct is important. As well as meeting and greeting your assessor, dealing effectively with contingencies that may arise will provide further opportunities to demonstrate your skills and abilities. Should anything go wrong, such as a witness being delayed or unavailable, your assessor will help you consider alternative arrangements, such as a telephone interview.

During the course of the day, your assessor may observe your interactions with colleagues, children and parents. Respond to people as you would usually. It will be clear to the assessor if you are putting on an act. Be your normal professional self, speak with confidence and do not panic! Do remember that you will not be given any indication by the assessor as to the outcome, so do not be disappointed at the lack of feedback. You will be surprised at how quickly the day flies by, and then you can relax!

C H A P T E R S U M M A R Y

This chapter links closely with Chapter 6 and should be read in conjunction with it. The chapter discusses how to prepare for the setting visit from the perspective of two EYP assessors, who throughout have woven a theme of identifying supporting evidence for achievement of the Standards. They highlight what an assessor is looking for and offer sound advice for your preparation. This chapter concludes discussion of the assessment process for achieving EYP Status, but the assessment process is not the end of the journey. As an EYP you will, as a Professional, continue to reflect on and improve your practice, as well as encouraging and sharing this reflective process with others.

Moving on

Chapter 8 looks at why you should engage in continuing professional development and what possible opportunities there are for this within the rapidly changing Early Years sector.

FURTHER READING

Though not focussed on settings visits by EYPS assessors the following three links provide useful background reading regarding preparing for inspection/assessment

http://readingroom.lsc.gov.uk/lsc/National/nat-planningandpreparingforinspection-gn.pdf and

http://www.teachernet.gov.uk/management/curriculumdelivery/ofstedinspections/preparing/

This is a book that considers the 5 Children Act outcomes as a focus for inspection:

Preparing for Inspection http://www.nurseryworld.co.uk/Books/

8 Continuing professional development for Early Years Professionals

CHAPTER OBJECTIVES

By the end of this chapter you should:
- have understood the importance of CPD and its central position within the workforce;
- have developed a wider understanding of developments and opportunities within the Early Years sector;
- have gained insight into how other EYPs are engaging with CPD and looking to the future;
- be committed to providing high-quality Early Years provision, so helping children achieve their potential and supporting parents and families.

CWDC has stated that a candidate gaining EYP Status is participating in 'the first stage in a continuum of professional development that will underpin their career' (CWDC, 2007a, p.2). This chapter considers why, as an EYP, you should engage with continuing professional development (CPD). It then looks at development opportunities for Early Years Professionals within the Early Years sector. Finally, three EYPs offer their perspective on how they hope to make an impact on the quality of Early Years provision through their roles as EYPs and what possible opportunities may lie ahead for their continuing professional development.

The importance of continuing professional development

Throughout this book, you have been encouraged to consider how, as an Early Years practitioner, you lead and support other practitioners to develop their practice and how you lead and support other practitioners within your wider role in partnership with families, carers and other professionals. This has required you to engage in a cycle of reflection upon your role, which has meant you have analysed and evaluated your actions or practice, so informing what your future actions or practice will be. You have undertaken this cycle of reflection to demonstrate evidence against the Standards for EYP Status and by doing this you have already engaged in continuing professional development. If the process of achieving Early Years Professional Status is to be just the start of your CPD, it is now prudent to consider how you can continue to develop as a reflective practitioner and what further opportunities for career development are open to you. CPD is therefore considered next in this section by Linda Fairlamb, who explores the importance of CPD and why you should, as a professional, engage in it. Linda is a Senior Staff Tutor for the Faculty of Education and works for the Open University in the North-East of England. She has extensive experience of appointing tutors to work on Open University CPD Master's level courses. In addition, she has offered CPD sessions for Open University tutors, and for practitioners drawn from all sectors of education. Linda explores the centrality of CPD to the Early Years practitioner here.

Continuing professional development

Working with young children in the Early Years environment today is one of the most stimulating and exciting areas of work, but at times the challenges must make it seem like you are more of a mountain climber. You put all of your energy and effort into scaling the heights of one set of statutory requirements or recommendations, only to think that you have reached the peak and satisfied all possible requirements, and you find new challenges waiting for you, new requirements and new directions. It is challenging and difficult, but working with children, and particularly young children, should always be like that: developing, changing and improving.

The real value of continuing professional development is that it allows practitioners to take control over their own careers and to some extent their own Early Years environment. It is important to keep in the forefront of your mind that CPD is about the actual change we make to practice, and is not just a series of courses, events or lectures. The focus should always be very firmly on the impact that the practitioner can make on their Early Years environment. Courses, events, books and research can all be very important; they can stimulate and direct, bringing you into contact with other practitioners in the same field and allowing you to develop and try out ideas. But remember that there is room for both a formal and an informal element to CPD, and the very best CPD will have a wide range of inputs, including external expertise and formal courses linked to Early Years activity. In other words, CPD is a very personal and reflective response to your individual workplace and setting. CPD and engaging reflectively with external changes are also becoming increasingly expected of practitioners: 'the current changes expect reflection of early years practitioners' (Paige-Smith and Craft, 2008, p.3).

CPD should be able to provide the following.

- *The opportunity to observe and be observed, to reflect on the observations and to adapt practice. It encourages dialogue between the observer and the observed.*

- *Peer support, through both the formal structure of courses and informal, everyday Early Years environment development support through colleagues.*

- *Ongoing activity or activities. CPD is continuous as well as continuing and involves the practitioner in a cycle of reflection on practice, adaptation of and development of practice, and then more reflection. Such reflection should continually change practice in the workplace, allowing the most successful strategies to develop.*

- *Opportunities to change how you behave in the Early Years environment. Well-thought-out reflection and development will be welcomed in the workplace. It is development which is not rooted in reflective practice which is resisted generally.*

- *The opportunity to work within teams to effect change.*

Practitioners in the Early Years environment should not be daunted by new initiatives or challenges. They have been bombarded by statutory requirements arguably more than any other sector, and they have developed and risen to the challenges. Crucially, CPD allows you, as a practitioner, to test, develop and if necessary challenge current thinking on Early Years strategies. It provides the opportunity to reflect, experiment, evaluate and develop, and it allows you in so doing to take control, empowering yourself and those working around you. CPD will certainly help you to steer a pathway through your career and improve your satisfaction through widening opportunities. It increases confidence and helps to develop the ability to self-assess and set realistic targets. By recognising your own strengths, you can improve your practice and offer more to those around you, applying this self-knowledge to the workplace and so improving the experience for both colleagues and young children in your care. Furthermore, it allows you to identify and focus on special interests (such as observation), which you can then take forward through research or courses, developing specialist expertise which will empower you to reflect further and have an impact on practice, implementing change in order to challenge, develop and improve.

You might be tempted just to see CPD as yet another challenge, but by taking an interest in this validation pathway you may be surprised by how much you have already achieved. By starting a reflective journal on your experiences and maintaining it for an extended period, you will be able to see the effect that the application of the principles outlined above can make in your work in the Early Years environment. Paige-Smith and Craft (2008) advocate extending the idea of a journal and using a variety of media to record your thinking and actions: 'images (digital) . . . may form a focus of reflection . . . sound recordings, collected by adults and also by children . . . transcriptions of what children have said in conversation with one another and with practitioners'. However you see your journal developing, it should form a record of all of your activities and reflections and identify needs and activities; perhaps most importantly, you can recognise your own progress. It is better to be able to say honestly 'I am a practitioner with five years' experience' than to be a practitioner with one year's experience, repeated 15 times.

The next section looks at developments within the Early Years sector and how the role of the EYP relates to them.

Looking ahead: identifying possible career pathways for EYPs

The expansion of what were first known as Sure Start Children's Centres seeks to ensure that over 3,500 Children's Centres will be in operation by 2010. Their aim will be to offer every family, regardless of geographical location, 'access to high quality integrated services in their community' (NCSL, 2007). This integrated, multi-agency approach will provide care, family support, health services and early education services, all of which are seen as key to raising the quality of provision for children and their parents. CWDC does not intend, but does not rule out, that EYPs could, in addition to their fundamental role of implementing the Early Years Foundation Stage, manage these highly organised, multi-disciplinary Children's Centres. It remains a possibility, most particularly for EYPs in smaller integrated settings, that they could become the setting's leader and also its EYP.

The National Standards for Children's Centre leaders (settings leaders) are distinct from, but complementary to, the Standards for candidates who wish to achieve Early Years Professional Status. The two roles are seen as compatible and essential to ensure that Children's Centres fulfil their stated aim. Whilst an EYP will be seen as an 'agent of change to improve practice in the setting' (CWDC, 2007a, p.4), the award of the National Professional Qualification in Integrated Centre Leadership (NPQICL) will be made to those leaders who 'understand children's development needs, develop a detailed knowledge of the community in which they work, and deliver flexible responsive services which meet local needs' (NSCL, 2007).

A small number of candidates in the pilot phase for EYP status at the Open University were also enrolled on the pilot programme for award of NPQICL at Pen Green. One of these candidates, Ann Hume, is now both an EYP and a Children's Centre leader holding the NPQICL qualification. Ann has written a case study in Section 3 where she explores her vision of what impact she can make to the quality of Early Years provision in her dual role of being an EYP and a Children's Centre leader.

It is opportune now to consider, alongside the increase in the number of Children's Centres, the expansion in the numbers of EYPs (and Children's Centre leaders) that will be required to meet demand. Local authorities are requested to develop networks of EYPs through which EYPs will help to encourage and support recruitment to the role of EYP as well as influence Early Years practice and provision within the authority. CWDC offers support packages to local authorities to enable this initiative to be implemented successfully. At a regional CWDC meeting (12 March 2008), local authorities reported that this initiative had already led to some interesting developments. In one network, EYPs were hosting the meetings in rotation, so enabling network members to visit and observe practice in other settings. In another network, EYPs were discussing projects they had implemented in their setting and then analysing the potential for them to be the basis of action research as part of their CPD. Another network of EYPs had drawn up plans to offer targeted support to settings where practice needed to be improved. This initiative, as illustrated, allows for a multiplicity of CPD opportunities for EYPs, such as 'to contribute to the development of the EYP programme both locally and nationally' (CWDC, 2007d). In addition to the examples outlined above, opportunities are emerging for EYPs to deliver training within and beyond their own local authorities and to act as mentors to EYPs new to the role and also those who aspire to the role. These networks can be considered as communities of practice, that is communities whose members join together and 'share a concern or a passion for something they do and learn how to do it better as they interact regularly' (Wenger, 2008). The engagement with other professionals within such a community fosters the growth of both inter-professional practice and reflective practice and reinforces the notion of a professionalised workforce. Networks of EYPs will therefore be of significant importance to the improvement in provision of high-quality education and care for young children both across and between local authorities.

Many providers of pathways to achieving EYP Status are keen to recruit EYPs to both the role of mentor and the role of assessor. A mentor is someone who advises and supports someone (their mentee) who is new to a role or aspiring to achieve a role. In becoming a mentor on an EYP pathway you would be expected to be a reflective practitioner and encourage and develop this in your mentees. Further, you could create a community of mentors with possibilities of researching and promoting mentoring as part of your CPD. The role of an assessor with a provider offers tremendous opportunities for CPD. Not only will the provider offer opportunities for CPD as part of its commitment to its staff, but you will be at the forefront of assessing all the components of assessment on a pathway to achieving EYP Status. As an emerging EYP yourself you are best placed to recognise those skills, characteristics and effective practice that make the role of the EYP a crucial one within the workforce. In becoming an assessor and in being an EYP, you will be at the cutting edge of being able to 'define the environment', as discussed by Linda Fairlamb above.

One further opportunity to be considered here is that of joining a professional association and becoming part of establishing a professional identity for EYPs. Aspect (the Association of Professionals in Education and Children's Trusts) has created an EYP national committee to address a range of concerns in relation to the professionalisation of the Early Years workforce. This will include lobbying for a suitable national pay framework for EYPs and for specific programmes of CPD designed to assist EYPs' ongoing skills enhancement and future career progression. This is an exciting development. Further details are listed at the end of this chapter.

What follows in the next section are three case studies written by EYPs. In them they discuss how they see the role of an EYP impacting on their practice and how the role may develop in the future.

Meet three EYPs as they share their thoughts and practice

The first case study offered is by Ann Hume. Ann is an EYP and holds the National Professional Qualification in Integrated Centre Leadership. She works at Kingsway Children's Centre in Scunthorpe.

CASE STUDY

Ann Hume

My career in childcare has spanned 30 years. Over this time I have had the opportunity to work with a wide and varied number of services and agencies. Continuous professional development throughout my career has played an important role in enabling me to provide environments in which people can thrive. The delivery of services that provide effective outcomes for children and families has been at the core of everything that I have undertaken.

This has culminated in my most recent professional development, achieving both Early Years Professional Status (EYPS) and the National Professional Qualification in Integrated Centre Leadership (NPQICL), which is a graduate-level qualification.

I completed the EYPS through the Validation Pathway from September to December 2006. Between October 2006 and July 2007 I also completed the NPQICL.

After reading through both course outlines I felt that they would complement each other and a lot of the evidence gathered for the 39 Standards of the EYPS would meet the criteria of the NPQICL. My feelings were confirmed early on in my studies. The EYPS proved to be an excellent tool in developing my reflective ability. It proved to be invaluable in both my studies and my workplace environment. Reflection is a very powerful tool that enables continuous assessment, evaluation and performance management to become embedded in work practice.

In addition, my communication skills have been enhanced through completing the EYPS. Being reflective has developed my ability to take a step back and view things from a different perspective. I proactively encourage consultation and discussion, promoting engagement from others. The result has been effective outcomes in a more diverse, inclusive and enabling environment.

I feel that the introduction of the Early Years Professional Status and graduate-level qualifications into the Early Years sector is a really positive strategy that will raise the profile of childcare as a profession. Historically childcare has been viewed as the poor relation to other professions, and salaries have reflected this. In the future perhaps this can be redressed and parity achieved to attract a more diverse workforce.

These improvements will impact on the standards and quality of provision, ensuring that children and families are provided with services that meet their needs and support their well-being.

My vision for the future is a skilful, knowledgeable and highly qualified workforce that attracts the professional respect that it deserves. I feel that I have a significant role to play within the development of the childcare workforce and the development of services within my region in the future. The EYPS and NPQICL will enable me to do so. I anticipate that both of these new initiatives will take time to be recognised and fully utilised within the workforce. Any impact will not be able to be measured for many years to come. It will be work in progress.

I am however confident that there is a very bright future on the horizon for Early Years that will benefit the workforce, children and families for many generations to come.

This next case study is written by Sarah Presswood, who followed the Validation Pathway and achieved EYP Status in February 2007. Sarah works as an EYP at a nursery in Birmingham. It is an established private day nursery owned by a local charity. The nursery is registered for 47 places, and there is a staff of 15. In this case study Sarah reflects on how achieving EYP Status has made a difference to her role and what opportunities she feels are now available to her.

Sarah Presswood

As someone who feels as though they fell into being an Early Years practitioner rather than actively seeking out that path, when I heard about the role of an Early Years Professional I thought 'Yes, something to achieve, to prove I know what I am talking about.' I thought it would be something to give me credibility and status. For me it was more about having the title than what the process of gaining it would do for me. It is only now that I am an EYP and I have undergone that process that I fully understand what CWDC mean by EYP Status being to the EYP 'the first stage in a continuum of professional development that will underpin their career' (CWDC, 2007a).

Since gaining my EYP Status I have found myself asking not only 'What could be next?' but more importantly 'What should be next?' The process of gaining EYP status is very reflective – especially having gained it through the Validation Pathway. I needed to investigate my own practice and discover what was good about it. That process in itself has been one of the most valuable pieces of CPD I have ever undertaken. I would say that now I am a very reflective practitioner and increasingly find myself reviewing practices within my setting and urging other staff to do the same. This is where I feel that EYP Status has given me credibility. I don't mean people look at me and say 'She's an EYP. She must know what she's talking about.' I mean that I personally feel as though I have credibility. I do have something of value to contribute. That alone is valuable, but it's not enough. So 'What should be next?'

This continuum of CPD has made me ask 'Why am I an Early Years Professional and what do I want or hope to achieve?' I believe passionately in giving young children the opportunity to develop and be the best that they can be; that is how I 'fell' into becoming an Early Years practitioner. I wanted this opportunity for my children and for other children and felt that I could at that time make a difference. How then can I now be a facilitator of opportunities for other young children?

My current role as manager of a day nursery does provide me with some opportunities – by providing access to activities for young children who otherwise may never get to dress up, play with gloop, build a den or share time with other young children. However, I know this is not enough. I alone cannot provide all the opportunities that a young child will need. Again this is where being a reflective practitioner begins to impact on my practice. I realise I don't want to manage the nursery; I want to lead it. By definition 'leading' mean you are going somewhere; you have to have a destination. My destination is a place where I can make an enduring difference to the lives of young children and their families. I further realise that I will only be able to reach my destination by working with other professionals.

My experience tells me that parents can find parenting very challenging and that they are eager for help and support. Sometimes they will look for this support from the nursery, and this means that the Early Years practitioners within the setting have to be able to meet this need. I see this as very much a part of the role of an EYP – to be able to develop the competencies of the staff within their setting and even beyond. It is widely held that standards amongst the childcare workforce need to be raised; historically the workforce has been made up of young, not particularly academic, women who have perhaps been encouraged to see childcare as a less demanding occupation. This should never have been the case – caring for and educating young children should never be described as anything but demanding and challenging.

Thus, for me, raising these standards amongst the workforce could be a very real opportunity as an EYP. As I have already said, undertaking the EYP Validation Pathway has made me more of a reflective practitioner, who reflects on not only my practice but the practices within the setting as a whole, and this has caused me to actively seek ways of changing our practice and supporting the staff to develop their own practice. This then is again part of the continuum of CPD – I have to develop my own understanding and practice to support the development of my staff and their practice. This can be done in a variety of ways, including reading, attending training courses and linking up with other professionals for advice and expertise.

Working with or alongside other professionals within the Early Years sector should be seen as another possible route for development for an EYP, whether it is by using the understanding gained from the EYP process about the many other agencies that can be engaged to improve the outcomes for children and their families and then using their expertise to enhance the services offered by the setting, or by working within a multi-disciplinary team to provide ready access to the many services that a young family may need. One avenue for development in this area could be to work as an EYP within a Children's Centre – this would be in line with the government's aim to have an EYP in every Children's Centre by 2010; in addition it would allow me to expand on my role by working with a much larger team of practitioners as part of the integrated services Children's Centres must offer.

I know for me that gaining EYPS definitely has been 'the first step' in my continuing professional development. It has presented me with opportunities to make that difference that I have believed in for so long. Some of the opportunities I have had to create for myself by reflecting on and refining my own practice. Some of the opportunities have come from unexpected sources. I have been asked to reflect on and write about my experiences and share them with others in a variety of ways. One such way has been to write a monthly article for Nursery World *magazine on leadership. Before gaining EYP Status, I hadn't always thought of myself or of my role as being a 'leader', but now I know I am expected to influence practice through leadership and support of colleagues.*

I hope that the insights I share through these articles resonate with and inspire others to 'lead' their co-workers to achieve better outcomes and to become EYPs. I have also taken part in EYP assessor training by offering insight into the assessment process from a candidate's point of view. I enjoyed being part of this event and hope to be asked to take part again. It is exciting – I am making a difference.

Anna Corbett, a Full-training Pathway candidate, has written this case study, where she reflects on how she was drawn to becoming an EYP and her experiences during her placements.

CASE STUDY

Anna Corbett

I was first attracted to work in Early Years as a result of completing various child development modules for my degree at Sheffield Hallam University. I have a great interest in the ways in which young children learn and develop and know how critical the first five years can be in a child's development. I knew this was a career I wanted to pursue and one I would find both enjoyable and rewarding.

I was initially attracted to teaching and was considering completing a PGCE in primary education when I heard through the National Day Nurseries Association about the opportunity to become an EYP. I hadn't heard much about EYPs up until that point, so I decided to research this to see if it was something I would be interested in. After reading information about EYP Status I was confident that this would suit me better than a PGCE, as I would be able to take on the role of a leader and really make a difference to young children's learning.

I applied for the full-time training pathway, as although I had some knowledge in child development I had very little 'hands on' experience. I was very pleased to be accepted on to the pathway, and I was enrolled on to a level 5 introductory diploma in management to support my gaining of leadership skills.

I was required to carry out two work placements in different settings, and very much enjoyed the first one. This was a pre-school setting, and I was there for 12 weeks. I was a bit apprehensive at first, as I had no experience in this type of environment, but by the end of it I felt confident I could go into my second setting with a good knowledge of effective practice and the soon-to-be-introduced Early Years Foundation Stage. I then commenced my second placement in a private day nursery offering provision from birth to 5.

As part of the pathway I was studying courses E123 and E124 (the Certificate in Early Years Practice) with the Open University. I really enjoyed these courses and found they provided much-needed support for my practice and further strengthened my understanding of Early Years care and education.

From the moment I started my placement in the second setting I asked the manager if I could be involved in all aspects of practice, including planning. After I had been there for around two weeks I was approached by the owner, who was interested to know how I was getting on with the course and any future plans I had. It was during this conversation that she asked if I would like to take on the position of deputy manager. I said yes straight away! I considered this to be a fantastic opportunity for me to develop my new skills and be able to engage more with the setting and bring fresh ideas.

I will be able to draw on my training for this post in various ways. The leadership and management skills I have gained will prove invaluable for me, and I know I can draw on my extensive knowledge of observation techniques and lead the other practitioners to carry out skilled observations. I will also be involved in planning of the curriculum, and the Open University study has provided me with much knowledge on how to do this and how to relate planning to individual children.

In the future I would like to continue my professional development by working in a Children's Centre, as I am extremely keen to get involved in providing integrated education and care for families while working alongside other professionals.

I consider myself to be extremely lucky to have come straight out of university with a clear vision of my future career plans, while having fantastic job satisfaction.

CHAPTER SUMMARY

This is not meant to be the final chapter to the completion of the Validation Pathway but to be the first chapter of what comes next. This chapter has encouraged you, as a professional, to engage with your continuing professional development and has set out possible opportunities for this development within the Early Years sector. It has drawn on three candidates' experiences of working to achieve EYP Status and how they feel now as part of the graduate-led workforce within the expanding Early Years sector. Chapter 1 concluded by saying 'This is a time of change, of challenge and of commitment; it is about becoming an EYP.' Now, as an EYP, you are accepting change, you know the challenge and you are demonstrating commitment. There has never been a more exciting time for being an Early Years Professional than now.

Moving on

The following may be of interest as you consider how to continue with your professional development.

- For more information about the EYP Section of Aspect, the Association of Professionals in Education and Children's Trusts, visit http://www.aspect.org.uk.

- To read more about leadership and management in the Early Years, consider the book *Leadership and Management in the Early Years: From Principles to Practice*, by Caroline Jones and Linda Pound (2008), published by McGraw-Hill, Maidenhead.

- To learn more about Etienne Wenger and his work on communities of practice, visit http://www.ewenger.com/theory/index.htm.

References

Ball, C (1994) *Start Right: The Importance of Early Learning*. London: RSA.

Brock, A (2006) Dimensions of early years professionalism – attitudes versus competences? Reflection Paper from Training Advancement and Cooperation in Teaching Young Children (TACTYC). **http://www.tactyc.org.uk/pdfs/Reflection_brock.pdf** (accessed 12 January 2008).

Clark, MM and Waller, T (2007) *Early Childhood Education and Care*. London: Sage.

CWDC, Children's Workforce Development Council (2006a) **http://www.cwdcouncil.org.uk/ aboutcwdc/whatwedo** (accessed 23 January 2008).

CWDC, Children's Workforce Development Council (2006b) *A Head Start for All*. London: CWDC.

CWDC, Children's Workforce Development Council (2007a) *Guidance to the Standards for the Award of Early Years Professional Status*. London: CWDC.

CWDC, Children's Workforce Development Council (2007b) *Candidates' Handbook: A Guide to the Gateway Review and Assessment Process*. London: CWDC.

CWDC, Children's Workforce Development Council (2007c) *Providers' Handbook: A Guide to the Gateway Review and Assessment Process*. London: CWDC.

CWDC, Children's Workforce Development Council (2007d) **http://www.cwdcouncil.org.uk/ projects/eyp_la_support.htm** (accessed 16 February 2008).

CWDC, Children's Workforce Development Council (2008) **http://www.cwdcouncil.org.uk/ news/detail.asp?news=EYPs+establish+National+Committee** (accessed 16 February 2008).

DCSF, Department for Children, Schools and Families (2007) *The Children's Plan: Building Brighter Futures*. **http://www.dcsf.gov.uk/publications/childrensplan/downloads/ Childrens_Plan_Executive_Summary.pdf** (accessed 15 February 2008).

DCSF, Department for Children, Schools and Families (2008a) *The Early Years Foundation Stage*. Nottingham: DfES Publications.

DCSF, Department for Children, Schools and Families (2008b) *Practice Guidance for the Early Years Foundation Stage*. Nottingham: DfES Publications.

DCSF, Department for Children, Schools and Families (2008c) *Statutory Framework for the Early Years Foundation Stage*. Nottingham: DfES Publications.

DfEE, Department for Education and Employment (2001) *EYDCP Planning Guidance 2001*. Nottingham: DfEE Publications.

DfES, Department for Education and Skills (2003) *Every Child Matters*. Nottingham: DfES Publications.

DfES, Department for Education and Skills (2005a) *Common Core*. Nottingham: DfES Publications.

DfES, Department for Education and Skills (2005b) *Key Elements of Effective Practice*. Nottingham: DfES Publications.

DfES, Department for Education and Skills (2006) Common Assessment Framework. http://www.everychildmatters.gov.uk/deliveringservices/caf (accessed 16 February 2008).

DfES, Department for Education and Skills (2007a) http://www.standards.dfes.gov.uk/eyfs/site/about/index.htm (accessed 23 January 2008).

DfES, Department for Education and Skills (2007b) *Every Parent Matters*. http://www.teachernet.gov.uk/wholeschool/familyandcommunity/workingwithparents/everyparentmatters (accessed 22 February 2008).

HM Treasury (2004) *Choice for Parents, the Best Start for Children: A Ten Year Strategy for Childcare*. London: HM Treasury.

NCSL, National College for School Leadership (2007) http://www.ncsl.org.uk/aboutus/pressreleases/pr-26022007.cfm (accessed 16 February 2008).

Ofsted, Office for Standards in Education (2007) Inspection of early years provision from September 2008. www.ofsted.gov.uk (accessed 23 January 2008).

Paige-Smith, A and Craft, A (eds) (2008) *Developing Reflective Practice in the Early Years*. Maidenhead: Open University Press.

Paige-Smith, A, Craft, A and Craft, M (2008) Democratic reflective practice, in Paige-Smith, A and Craft, A (eds) *Developing Reflective Practice in the Early Years*. Maidenhead: Open University Press.

Rodd, J (2006) *Leadership in Early Childhood*. 3rd edition. Maidenhead: Open University Press.

Schön, DA (1973) *The Reflective Practitioner: How Professionals Think in Action*. London: Temple Smith.

Siraj-Blatchford, I and Manni, L (2006) *Effective Leadership in the Early Years Sector Study*. http://www.gtce.org.uk/shared/contentlibs/126795/93128/120213/eleys_study.pdf (accessed 12 January 2008).

Sure Start (2004) *Parents and Work: A Guide for Sure Start Local Programmes*. Nottingham: DfES.

Sylva, K, Melhuish, EC, Sammons, P, Siraj-Blatchford, I and Taggart, B (2004) *The Effective Provision of Pre-school Education (EPPE) Project: Final Report*. London: DfEE/Institute of Education, University of London.

Wenger, E (2008) http://www.ewenger.com/theory/index.htm (accessed 16 February 2008).

Index